Aromatherapy
The Essential Beginning

D. Gary Young, N.D.

Creator of
Essential Oil Formulas,
Food Supplements and
Skin Care Products

Published by Essential Press Publishing
P.O. Box 9282
Salt Lake City, UT 84109

For further information contact:
Young Living Essential Oils
250 South Main Street
Payson, UT 84651
1-800-763-9983

Printed in the United States of America

ISBN 0-9648187-0-1

Second Edition

About the Cover

Photograph taken from the wall of the Edfu Temple of the Priests in Upper Egypt. It depicts a priest making a ritual offering of **Lotus Oil.** Not only was this oil used for spiritual rituals, but also for medicinal purposes, and was the most prized oil in all of ancient Egypt. It was also used to ward off evil deities and was available only to the pharaohs and their hierarchy.

Preface

There are many dedicated people throughout the world who are studying the vast dimensions of Aromatherapy. The interest is growing dramatically as the benefits of essential oils are becoming more widely known, not only in the everyday household but also in the scientific world as more and more research is being done and becoming available to the public. Essential oils are the heartbeat of the plant kingdom and perhaps the most exciting life-giving substance we have in the world today. This heartbeat is the energy that was created to deliver the nutrients into every cell of the body with their ability to regenerate, strengthen and protect mankind.

The world of essential oils is a reawakening of our planet. We must have a respectful awareness and treat this information kindly so that it can continue to come forth and be used for our benefit. The pure intelligence of essential oils may be the only tool that can reach into the deep recesses of our brain, cross over the chemical barriers and open the hidden channels of our minds, allowing access to greater knowledge and discernment in reaching our higher potential to become more Christ-like, to communicate without speaking, to focus our thinking and to be able to manifest our thoughts into reality. We want to raise our frequency so we can heal ourselves and then help others heal themselves. Science is only now rediscovering these healing substances that were used in ancient times.

Chemical research shows that essential oils may even help create an environment in which disease, bacteria, virus, fungus, etc., cannot live. The ongoing research project which we began in 1995, with the chemistry department at Weber State University in Utah is continually validating my beliefs all along about the tremendous antimicrobial, antioxidant and antibacterial activity of our Singles and Blends. Everyone involved is excited about the positive results and is anxious for our findings to be published.

I know that this is just a beginning and that there are many who will help to bring this knowledge to the reality of the modern world. I am grateful to be a part of this great work and am dedicated to bringing the knowledge and power of essential oils back into our modern day. We at Young Living are committed to producing and selling the finest quality and purest oils in the world.

D. Gary Young, N.D.
Aromacologist

Forward

*T*he use of essential oils dates back to ancient times, but there has never been a time when essential oils are more needed than today. The world is facing a medical disaster.

Modern technology has produced the jet aircraft, which can be the instrument of transferring disease around the world in hours. The invasion of the rain forest has revealed new plagues that humanity never knew existed. The overuse of modern-day wonder drugs has created mutations that medical science never anticipated.

Medically, there has never been such a potentially hazardous time in all of history as there is in the world today. Fortunately, there are answers that provide a way for us to protect ourselves, our family and our friends from these potential dangers.

A number of years ago, Gary Young and I met when we were both speaking at the same seminar. I was fascinated by his lecture. His depth of knowledge of essential oils and nutrition exceeded anything I had ever heard on this subject.

I believe the Lord has again brought forth the knowledge of essential oils for man's use so that he might be spared from the inevitable medical disaster that looms on the horizon. I hope that people everywhere will open their minds to the resurgence of knowledge and use of essential oils and have their blessed benefits.

Gary Young is to be congratulated for bringing these truths forth in such an excellent book as this. I know of no one else who has excelled in formulating products that will meet our needs and supply the necessary nutrients to help us build and maintain healthy bodies to protect us in these perilous times.

This forward would not be complete without saying that I have used Gary Young's essential oil products for some time, and I would not want to be without them. They are the purest and finest that I have found anywhere.

I consider it a privilege to have this book in my library, and I am sure that we will see the day when this information may save millions of lives.

Lindsey Williams
Author

Dedication

I dedicate this book to those who are seeking greater knowledge
in their quest to help heal themselves and this beautiful earth
on which we live and to all the true pioneers
in the field of aromatherapy.

Acknowledgements

I wish to express my love, appreciation and heartfelt thanks to:

Mary Young, my beautiful and loving wife, for her unwavering faith and constant encouragement, even when I felt the task was too much with everything else. Her unending strength and long hours at the computer, sometimes 16 -18 hours a day typing, editing and adding new information that I was continuously writing, made this book possible.

Alene Frandsen for editing, proofing and helping Mary for countless hours. Her reliability and dedication also made it possible to focus on the writing of this book, knowing that all was well at the office.

Dr. Brenton G. Yorgason and Professor Cyrus McKell for their support, encouragement, editing skills and great friendship.

LaRue Billeter, my Mother-In-Law, who took over the gardening and care of our home so Mary had time to type and who was always so willing to run errands and take care of so many little time-consuming things.

Bruce Tainio for all the help he has been to me in the development of the farm and for the nutritional products he developed for the soil as well as all that he has taught me about frequency.

We especially want to thank Paul Springer for his terrific design work and Robin Sheppick who worked late hours to format this book. Their personal interest and diligent work beyond the call of duty created wonderful teamwork at the graphic art design company of Bailey-Montague & Associates in preparing this book in such a timely fashion.

And last, but not least, I want to thank all of my friends and family members who kept encouraging me and who labored in the fields at the Young Living Research Farm so I could have the time to complete the writing of this book.

Table of Contents

Aromatherapy: An Ancient Science Returns to the Modern World

The Essential Beginning

"Moreover, the Lord spoke unto Moses saying:
Take thou also unto thee principal spices of pure myrrh...
of sweet cinnamon...of sweet calamus...of cassia...and of olive...
and thou shalt make it an oil of holy ointment,
an ointment compound after the art of the apothecary:
it shall be an holy anointing oil."

EXODUS 30:22-25

*A*ccording to the translation of ancient Egyptian hieroglyphics and Chinese manuscripts, priests and physicians were using oils thousands of years before the time of Christ. There are 188 references to oils in the *Bible.* Some precious oils, such as frankincense, myrrh, galbanum, rosemary, hyssop, cassia, cinnamon and spikenard, were used for the anointing and healing of the sick. Additionally, biblical prophets recognized the use of essential oils as a protection for their bodies against the ravages of disease.

By way of illustration, the wise men brought the oils of frankincense and myrrh to the Christ child. Clinical research now shows that frankincense oil contains very high immune-stimulating properties. The ancient process of oil distillation is a delicate and precise art that has almost been forgotten. Science is just now rediscovering the healing substances of essential oils that were used in ancient times, and beginning to acknowledge their value. Young Living Essential Oils is helping to bring history to life through research and essential oil formulations in order to restore this ancient knowledge to our modern world.

On February 8, 1973, while homesteading 300 acres of beautifully timbered land in Canada, I was seriously injured in a logging accident. This accident resulted in multiple fractures, and according to the medical specialists, I was confined to a wheelchair and paralyzed for life. After nearly two years of severe pain and depression, I decided to take action and regain control of my life. I began to research and study, and then apply various methods of alternative healing, thus beginning my gradual regeneration. Over a period of two years, I went from a wheelchair to a walker, then to crutches, and finally to walking – but not without considerable pain. In 1982, after receiving a master's degree in Nutrition and a doctorate in Naturopathy, I opened a clinical family practice in Chula Vista, California, as well as a research clinic in La Mesa, Mexico.

In 1983, I studied the research on Tea Tree Oil and incorporated it into my practice for use with cuts, bruises, burns, pain, etc. However, one year later, I was very disappointed with the poor results. I read other research and information on essential oils, but never really became excited about them until I was invited to attend a medical seminar being held at the Medical University in Geneva, Switzerland. This seminar was taught by medical doctors Jean Claude Lapraz, M.D., and Paul Duraffourd, M.D., on the treatment of respiratory disease with essential oils. The lectures were very stimulating, and opened new thoughts on therapeutic approaches. I returned to my clinic with 13 oils and great anticipation. The first year I conducted research on lab animals, a few patients and did various blood studies. The research results were amazing in that I discovered how the oils could increase cellular oxygen and promote immune function. This was also my first discovery of poor oil quality. I later learned that the Tea Tree oil that was sold in America, and which I was using in my clinic, was 4th and 5th grade quality. When I purchased 1st grade quality Tea Tree Oil, or melaleuca as it is also called, I could clearly see definitive results.

Annemarie Buhler introduced me to the world of essential oils, and encouraged me to learn more about them. She traveled with me to Switzerland and France to help me study and investigate the world of Aromatherapy. Her support and influence, for which I will ever be grateful, contributed greatly to the direction of my life's work.

While I was most interested in helping my patients, I had not thought of how my own health might benefit from the oils. It had been 13 years since my accident, and I still suffered with pain. Likewise, I had great limitations, as I had the ability to walk only short distances. One morning, awakening with intense pain, the thought came to me to use the oils on myself. I did, and within three days, I was walking without pain. One week later, I was jogging for the first time in 13 years. Then, in November of 1986, I entered a half-marathon and finished in 60th place out of 970 participants!

As one might well understand, this remarkable recovery propelled me with even greater speed and intensity into discovering the benefits of essential oils and learning how to use them.

I gained my first training in essential oils from Jean Claude Lapraz, M.D., in 1985 at the Medical University in Geneva, Switzerland. From there I went on to Paris to study with Paul Belaiche, M.D., one of two leading French physicians conducting research on essential oils. At this time Dr.

Belaiche was teaching the chemistry properties and introducing people to the wonderful world of oils. From there I traveled to England to study with various doctors and to do essential oil research at the Warwick University and the University of London. I spent long hours in the British Museum Library and the Library of London where I researched the foundation and history of essential oils. I studied with Daniel Pénoël, M.D., who was a student of Jean Valnet, M.D. Dr. Valnet was the first medical doctor to conduct research and to write about the medical application of essential oils in our modern times. Dr. Pénoël and the French chemist, Pierre Franchomme, have contributed greatly to the scientific research and documentation of the therapeutic value and importance of essential oils. Their published findings have been invaluable to those desiring scientific and medical information. Together they wrote *L'aromathérapie exactement,* the Aromatherapy medical textbook and encyclopedia. This text gave us the description, definition and prescribing application of 86 different essential oils with their properties responsible for their antiviral, antibacterial, antifungal, anti-infectious and immune-stimulating activities.

I will forever be grateful for my friendship with Philippe Mailhebiau and his staff, Oliver Clec, Dr. Jean Marc Soulier and Dr. Jacqueline Azémar. Philippe is the owner of the French government certified laboratory, Phytosun'Arôms. He is an author and lecturer, and one of the few in the world who is a gifted "Nose." He and his staff have taught me much, and have always been willing to share their knowledge, research and expertise with me.

In 1990, I met Jean-Noël Landel, with whom I became partners in a research farm in southern France. We started with 12 acres, which has now grown to 320. He and his wife, Jane, are wonderful friends and open their home to me whenever I am there. Jean-Noël has spent many years in the study of essential oils, and is an expert at growing and distilling, as well as being dedicated to protecting our interests in oil quality.

Kurt Schnaubelt, Ph.D., the owner and founder of the Pacific Institute of Aromatherapy, has been a marvelous tutor for me in the field of oil chemistry. I have learned much from him and continue to enjoy his friendship. He has always promoted the use of pure, unadulterated oils.

Over the past three years, I have studied at Cairo University under Radwan Farag, Ph.D. Dr. Farag is the head of the biochemistry department, and has written and published 92 research papers on essential oils. He has received more awards than any other human being in the world in this field of study. Dr. Farag documented the **oxygenating molecular activity** in essential oils, and was responsible for the discovery of their **antioxidant and antimicrobial activity.** He was a guest speaker at the Young Living Essential Oils annual conference, in 1994, and has participated with me in joint research in the study of essential oils for the prevention of degenerative disease.

Dr. Farag with Dr. Young in the Young Living Laboratory, January 1994.

Dr. Young at the Cairo University Agriculture Facility while doing research with Dr. Farag.

I have studied in these various countries to gain the knowledge that would enable me to spread the importance of essential oils throughout the world. Invaluable time was spent studying at the Hebrew University in Jerusalem, identifying the historical association in the *Bible* with the life of Christ – and His connection to essential oils and what He might have passed on to His disciples. Israel was a major producer of oils during the time of Christ, even up until 10 years ago when they gave up the processing and distilling of oils. They did this because the terrorist activity and contention in their country made it difficult for the export business. There is so much history of essential oils in that country; but with the fighting and turmoil there, it becomes very difficult to spend time to conduct research there.

Throughout the world, there is a lot of research to be conducted on essential oils and the art of distillation. The more we can learn from history, the faster our growth will be in understanding and learning how to use essential oils.

Ancient Aromas

*A*roma is the oldest means of reaching and influencing the deepest human instincts. When we examine creation, we find that everything from dust to man has an odor. Ancient Indian philosophy was often quoted as saying, "The fragrance of a flower travels with the wind, but the odor of a holy man travels against the wind." Early Christian historians attached specific smells to various saints. St. Catherine smelled of violets, St. Theresa of jasmine, St. Lydwine of cinnamon, and St. Francis of Assisi of lemon. Many of the Tibetan monks recognized people's intentions and habits by their body odors. Ancient physicians diagnosed disease by the individual's odor.

The famous French detective Vidocq stated, "If I am in a crowd of over 1,000 people, I can single out every violator of the moral law by the smell." He stated that every area of criminal activity has its own odor, and he could identify each one.

The ancient ones had so fully explored the mysteries of odor and fragrance that in many ways their lives and life styles depended on it.

Many writings and suggestions tell where the use of essential oils began. Some say that Aromatherapy began in China, some in India. Even so, my research reveals that Egyptian civilization created and developed many of the more technical advances in society insofar as machinery, architecture, structural building and medicine are concerned. Of course, we read about embalming the bodies of pharaohs and queens, and know that the ancient Egyptian people had incredible knowledge of anatomy, surgery and medicine.

During the Neolithic period, it was discovered that fatty oils could be extracted from the olive tree through the process of pressing. These oils were used to protect the skin from the sun, and to keep the hair from becoming dry and brittle. They were also used for curing and tanning hides for making clothing, as well as for cooking and bathing.

The Egyptians were the first to discover the potential of fragrance. They created various fragrances for the individual's personal benefit, as well as for rituals and ceremonies performed in the temples and pyramids. According to records dating back to 4500 B.C., they were also using balsamic substances with aromatic properties in religious rituals and for medicines. Translations of ancient writings tell of scented barks and resins of spices and aromatic vinegars, wines and beers that were used in rituals, temples, astrology, embalming and medicine. Three oils used in the embalming process were cedarwood, myrrh and frankincense.

The translation of ancient papyrus found in the Temple of Edfu reveal which aromatic substances were blended to specific formulation by the alchemist and the high priest in order to make medicinal formulas and perfume recipes for their rituals. Many of these substances were originally crushed and steeped with olive oil. They would take cedar bark, strip it, grind it fairly fine, soak it with olive oil, wrap it in a wool cloth, and then burn the cloth. The heat of the cloth would pull the essential oil out of the bark into the olive oil. They would then press the wool cloth and extract the oil in that fashion. They found that by placing petals in goose or goat fat, the fat would work as a catalyst to extract the oil. The oil was then separated from the fat. This was the first technique called "absolute," which was an extraction without steam.

The Egyptian high priests understood the value of fragrances for opening the subconscious mind and elevating their ability to communicate with their spirit world. They used exotic aromas on their congregations to promote a greater state of tranquility. One of the favorite perfumes used by the Egyptians was Kyphi, which was believed to contain a mixture of 16 different oils, including myrrh, juniper, frankincense, jasmine and rose.

In 1817, the Ebers Papyrus was discovered. It was over 870 feet long, and was referred to as a medicinal scroll. It dated back to 1500 B.C., and included over 800 different formulations of herbal prescriptions and remedies. Other scrolls indicated that the Egyptians had a very high success rate in treating 81 different diseases. Many mixtures contained myrrh, oil and honey. Myrrh is still recognized for its ability to help with infections of the skin and throat, and to regenerate skin tissue. Because of its effectiveness in preventing bacterial growth, myrrh was also used for embalming.

In 1922, when King Tut's tomb was opened, 350 liters of oils were discovered in alabaster jars. Plant waxes had solidified into a thickened residue around the inside of the container openings, leaving the liquefied oil in excellent condition.

The ancient Egyptians and Babylonians believed that in order to reach a realm of higher spirituality, they had to be clean and beautiful. They practiced fumigation as a means for disbursing oils to purify the air around them – thus, protecting them from evil spirits. They also believed that purifying and beautifying their bodies made them more pleasing to the gods, and that if they kept their bodies clean and fragrant, they would enter the world beyond the grave in their earthly bodies.

History records that one of the founders of "pharaonic" medicine was the architect Imhotep, who was the Grand Vizier of King Zeser (2780 - 2720 B.C.). Imhotep is often given credit for ushering in the use of oils, herbs, and aromatic plants for medicinal purposes. The physicians of Ionia Attia and Crete came to the cities of the Nile to increase their knowledge. At this time, the school of Cas was founded, and was attended by Hippocrates (460 to 377 B.C.), whom the Greeks, in their enthusiasm and with some exaggeration, named the "Father of Medicine." We know that Hippocrates was not the Father of Medicine but rather was only a student who exploited and taught many of the remedies already being practiced.

The Celtics also proved to be some of the best doctors up to that time, and enriched themselves with knowledge from their Mediterranean colleagues. In about the 8th Century B.C., the Arabs, as both merchants and warriors, spread the remedies from Asia Minor to the Middle East, and focused their work on improving the method of extracting essential oils.

The Egyptian people started collecting essential oils and placing them in alabaster vessels. These vessels were specifically carved and shaped for housing scented oils. Many of their cosmetic formulas had a basis of goose grease and goat fat. They would make eye liners, eye shadows, and stain their hair and nails from a variety of ointments and perfumes. These applications were made from the same aromatic oils used in the temples, which were put in evaporation dishes for fragrancing the different rooms and chambers where their sacred work and rituals were performed.

In Search of The Blue Lotus

One of the most exotic oils of all times, sought after by all the kings and high priests, was the Blue Lotus. The White Lotus was also revered as the most treasured flower in all the land, and was depicted on the temple walls, tombs and pyramids throughout all of Egypt. The people of this great land – the high priests, and physicians – depended on the White Lotus to provide many of their daily needs. The kings, queens and pharaohs adorned themselves with the erotic perfume they extracted from its flower. The White Lotus was very prevalent throughout Egypt. It provided the foundation of medicine, as they discovered that this plant, particularly the roots, contained anti-cancerous properties. They also found that the leaf and stem helped prevent diabetes when made into a tea along with various other plants. Diabetes was the worst disease of that day, and was quite common among the ruling hierarchy. They had a sweet tooth; and with the sugar cane that was commonly grown there, in addition to the naturally sweet fruit which grew in abundance, they were accustomed to eating a lot of sweets. The Egyptians were not concerned with disease, and therefore didn't really feel a need to discipline their diets. They had the knowledge of diseases, but also knew how to treat and cure them.

The bulbs of the White Lotus, when dried and ground, provided a healthy and delicious flour for making bread and other foods. The stems, leaves and flowers provided various medicinal properties for healing; and, of course, the flowers provided the exotic perfume that was so loved by the people. The Lotus, papyrus and black cumin are depicted in the hieroglyphics in the temples. The Temple of Edfu was the temple for the priests, and the Temple of Denderah was the temple for priestesses. These two temples were the temples in which the people were taught how to heal with oils and herbs. Each temple had its own library, laboratory and apothecary. The Temple of Kom Ombo was the only temple ever built for both men and women. Here, medical students studied medicine, and were trained in the finer skills of surgery.

In my search for the Blue Lotus, I kept hearing about it everywhere. Even so, no one really seemed to know much about it, or where it could be found. They spoke only of the legends. I was fascinated as I watched their countenance change to show a very proud and respectful feeling as they talked about their heritage with the Blue Lotus.

When the archeologists opened the tombs of Ramses and Tutankhamon, they found particles that were believed to have been the Blue Lotus. This beautiful flower was engraved with gold, and the leaves were inlaid with stone on the sarcophagi of the great kings. It has been said that only the kings had access to the Blue Lotus Oil, and that this oil gave them great spiritual powers, as well as protected them from death. **The ancient legends said that those who possessed the Blue Lotus would never have sickness.** The Lotus was also used in religious rituals as offerings to their gods, thus giving them great favor and putting them in good standing. As a result, the gods would bless them with great wealth.

I traveled through Egypt for three years looking for the illusive Blue Lotus. I followed one story after another, and felt like I was chasing the end of a rainbow. After two years, I was almost convinced that it really didn't exist. Just before leaving Egypt in March of 1993, I was talking to a taxi driver at the airport about the Blue Lotus. He smiled and nodded his head in understanding. He then replied, "Everybody wants the Blue Lotus, and they all come to Cairo. The Blue Lotus doesn't grow in Cairo – only in upper Egypt by the high dam. My family talks about it a lot. The oil has very powerful healing abilities, and the ancestors worshiped it."

After the Ramses dynasties, the new King Akhenaton wanted to restore the belief that Moses taught about having only one God, stated simply, he wanted to end the worshipping of graven images, including the Blue Lotus. He ordered all the Lotus to be destroyed, thus bringing its life to a tragic and unnecessary end.

However, different relatives of the kings had been assigned to grow and care for the Lotus, and some of these families made an effort to keep it alive. As I would hear these stories, I would regain my hope, and again start chasing the rainbow. My return to Egypt in March of 1994 proved to be a history-making expedition. After completing several days of research at the university, I flew to Aswan, thinking I had some good leads. It was a hot day when I landed, and I asked several English speaking taxi drivers if they knew about the Lotus. One young man said he did, and that his grandfather knew the legend of the ancient people and could help. With my heart pounding through my shirt pocket, we were off to Aswan to locate a small mud brick house on the west side of the river just below the dam. I sat spellbound for four hours as the grandfather, in his eighties, talked about the history of the Blue Lotus. This he did while his grandson translated.

I soon learned that the Blue Lotus was grown in several remote areas along the Nile River, on small deltas and peninsulas, where they were hidden from the king. The grandfather told of how this plant healed tumors, blindness, baldness, stomach sicknesses, etc., that he had seen in his family when he was a child. One of the formulas I photographed on the wall at Denderah was for the liver, and was formulated with Lotus leaves, wine, powdered zizyphus, figs, juniper berries, frankincense, and sweet beer. "Demonic constipation" was cured with the Lotus leaves and other herbs of which this old gentleman spoke. I was mesmerized the entire time I was with him, and wished that this moment could last for at least a week longer.

He gave me the names of several people who could help me in my search. I was excited to begin this journey, and in four days found myself in Northern Israel near the Syrian border. I was in the Hula Valley on the Jordan River where the Blue Lotus had been growing until six years earlier when it supposedly died out. Undaunted in my search, I went from there to Tel Aviv University, then back to Egypt to float down the greater part of the Nile, following one lead after another. What a glorious day it was three weeks later when I set foot onto a little island on the delta north of Ashmun, and was allowed to see the Blue Lotus. When the old gentleman described the feeling I would have, he was not exaggerating. I sat down and cried with joy and reverence to see this beautiful flower that represented the heartbeat of this ancient people.

The Egyptians were a vain people, consumed with their looks and beauty. Various kings were responsible for sending expeditions to other countries to collect plants and trees from which oil and herbal extracts could be made. Queen Hatshepsut, who reigned during the 18th dynasty, commissioned the Royal Egyptian Navy to set sail along the East Coast of Africa to countries like Sudan and Somalia. This they did in order to gather trees, shrubs, and herbs for the cultivating and extraction of medicinal properties. The ancient Egyptians discovered oils and their aromatic uses for medicinal purposes long before the actual plant was studied in its herbal application and incorporated into the field of medicine.

It is easy to look back into history and see that essential oils are likely the oldest form of medicine known to man. It is evident that the Chinese were aware of aromatics, as sanskrit documents of 2000 B.C., recorded by the Emperor Kiwang-ti, indicate the use of opium, pomegranate, rhubarb and aromatic substances. This is the earliest record we have of the Oriental culture using oils. In Vedic writings dating back several thousand years, as well as in the Kuma Sutra, a spiritual book that includes sacred poetry, extensive instructions for beauty care suggest that the oil of sandalwood was a special favorite of the Indian people.

The Greeks also elaborated on the use of essential oils for hair, skin and body massage for the feet, jaws, joints, and perhaps in the preventing of arthritic-type symptoms. They believed that the perfume was heaven sent via a nymph attending Aphrodite, the Goddess of Love.

The Romans also played an important role in the history of essential oils. They were very much into fumigating and diffusing oils in their temples and political buildings. Additionally, they bathed in hot tubs scented with oils, and then enjoyed a fragrant massage with their favorite oils. The Romans used essential oils and perfumes with virtually every aspect of their culture, particularly with the care of their bodies. They used oils in their homes, on furniture, rugs, and even adorned their flags with them.

The people of the Byzantine Empire (330 A.D. to 1400 A.D.) were known to have become addicted to the use of fragrances about 1000 A.D. The Arabian people also began to study the chemistry of the aromatic properties that resulted in a refined development of distillation. This was first implemented in the extraction of rose oil and rose water, which were very popular in the Middle East at that time. Various crusades and expeditions brought aromatic plants and properties from one country to another. Kings would barter and buy land, gold, slaves and women with the oils that they had extracted even with their crude methods. Thus, oils were more valuable than gold.

The European community did not process or produce essential oils until the 12th century. At that time, they perfected their own manufacturing processes, and began working with the indigenous plants of the area. Although Medieval Europeans lost touch with personal cleanliness, which helped bring on the great plagues of the 13th and 14th centuries, essential oils were still known to the thieves who robbed the bodies of the dead and were not infected. These robbers, known as spice traders and perfumers, bathed in such oils as pine, frankincense, balsam, clove, cinnamon and rosemary.

In various chapters of Exodus, Leviticus and Numbers, in the Bible, we read about herbs and oils, and the recipe the Lord gave to Moses after the art of the apothecary. When Christ was born, the oils of myrrh and frankincense were brought to Him as a gift. Later, we read about Christ anointing with oil, and Mary Magdalene anointing Christ's feet at the Last Supper as she washed his feet with the oil of Spikenard. Judas asked her why she did not sell the expensive oil and give the money to the poor. When the body of Christ was taken off the cross, it was wrapped in linen cloth that had been soaked with myrrh oil and placed in the tomb. Myrrh was used because it was purifying and prevented decomposition.

Throughout the Old Testament and up to the time of Christ, there are numerous references to the value of oils. What happened to the information about these oils after Christ? Perhaps during the Dark Ages and the burning of the libraries in Alexandria and other places, much of this knowledge was lost. Only through the cosmetic and perfume industry did this valuable science begin to resurface. With the combined use of modern technology in the field of medical science, scientific research and the translation of ancient writings, we will be able to rediscover and add to our knowledge about these healing substances as the Creator meant for us to use them.

What is Aromatherapy?
The Science of Essential Oils

*A*romatherapy is a phrase coined by French cosmetic chemist, René-Maurice Gattefossé, Ph.D., in 1920. While working in his laboratory, Dr. Gattefossé had an accident that resulted in a third degree thermal burn of his hand and forearm. Intending to cool the burn, he saw that his colleague had just brought in a container from the cooler; so he plunged his arm into a vat of lavender oil, thinking it was water. To his surprise, the burning slowly decreased, and within a few moments stopped. Over a period of time, with the continual application of lavender oil, the burn healed completely without a trace of a scar. Through this experience, Dr. Gattefossé became very excited with the potential of the healing properties in aromatic substances. As a chemist, he analyzed the essential oil of lavender, discovering that it contained many substances referred to as chemical constituents, or chemical properties.

Dr. Gattefossé determined that essential oils, the aromatic substances in many flowers, trees, shrubs, herbs, bushes, roots, seeds, leaves, stems, and flowering petals, contained healing properties in its semi-oily resin. Thus, the ancient art of Aromatherapy began its re-entry into the modern world.

Dr. Gattefossé shared his experience with his colleague and friend, Dr. Jean Valnet, a medical doctor in Paris, France. A few years later, Dr.

Valnet experimented with essential oils during the post-war years of World War I, and experienced amazing results. During World War II, while serving as a medical physician in the French Army at the China Wall, treating war victims, he ran out of antibiotics and other medications. Because of his previous experiences, he reverted to using essential oils; and to his amazement, they had a powerful effect in reducing and even stopping the infection. He was thus able to save many of the soldiers who otherwise would have died even with antibiotics. This was an important event in the awakening and beginning of modern-day Aromatherapy.

Dr. Valnet had two medical students, Dr. Paul Belaiche and Dr. Jean Claude Lapraz, who did their internship with him. These men were largely responsible for expanding his work. These two young medical doctors picked up on Dr. Valnet's work in the early 1960s, and conducted research in the laboratories, while practicing medicine using essential oils. They discovered that essential oils contain antiviral, antibacterial, antifungal and antiseptic properties, as well as being powerful oxygenators with the ability to act as carrying agents in the delivery of nutrients into the cells. These physicians have contributed greatly in developing techniques for the treatment of infectious disease with essential oils. This they did through their research and writing of professional papers and books.

The wholeness and complexity of Aromatherapy gives it the potential to do what it does. If you take a geranium plant and tear the leaf or the stem, a clear liquid will appear. This liquid is a very subtle and volatile essence that exudes from the damaged tissues of the leaf. So it is with the human body. With a cut or scrape, we see the flow of blood from the opening in the skin.

One significant difference between blood and the plant liquid is the color. In the resin or oil being released from the plant, we find trace elements of nutrients, hormones, enzymes, vitamins, minerals, antibodies, and antifungal, antibacterial, anti-infectious, antiseptic, and immune-stimulating properties. One other key agent found present in that resin, which is so important for sustaining and regenerating, is **OXYGEN.** Oxygen molecules are part of the chemical elements of the resin, such as alcohols, phenols, esters, sesquiterpenes, terpinols, etc. Together, these chemicals create an essential oil.

The plant releases the oil in order to clean the break, kill the bacteria, and begin the regeneration process. When blood is released through broken skin, it is for the same purpose – to clean the wound, kill the bacteria, prevent infection, and begin the healing and regeneration process. A simple comparison of the plant and the human body shows us a precise similarity, as both the oil and the blood are the transporters of the fundamental nutrients necessary to feed and nurture the cells. Furthermore, essential oils have the ability in their chemical structure to penetrate the cell wall and transport oxygen and nutrients inside that cell. **Because they are antioxidants, essential oils have been found to help increase oxygen.** They contain oxygenating molecules, and therefore have the ability to increase cellular oxygen – thus giving more support to the immune system. It has been said that anyone who uses essential oils on a continuous basis has a stronger immune system. Research has shown that with their immune-stimulating properties, essential oils enhance and support the building of the immune system. This is true whether they are inhaled, or are rubbed on the body topically. Even those who contract a cold or the flu recover 70 percent faster using essential oils.

It has been said that when essential oils are diffused in the home, they have the ability to increase the atmospheric oxygen. They do this by releasing oxygenating molecules into the atmosphere. Oils increase ozone and negative ions in the home, which in turn inhibit bacteria growth. This prevents and destroys existing odors from mold, cigarettes, animals, etc. Essential oils have the electrical magnetic attraction to fracture the molecular chain of chemicals and take them out of the air. This process renders them non-toxic to the body. Scientists in the European countries have found that essential oils will bond to metallics and chemicals, and carry them out of the body. They do this by working as a natural chelator, inhibiting these toxic substances from staying in the tissues. These are all wonderful attributes of essential oils. Essential oils remove dust particles out of the air, and **when diffused in the home, can be the greatest air filtration system in the world.**

Essential oils have the oldest history of healing known to man. Many books and stories have been written, claiming that essential oils date back several thousand years. There is no way of knowing precisely when it all began. We just know that oils have been around since the beginning of recorded history as we know it.

Essential oils can be extracted from different parts of the plants or trees, such as from the seeds, flowers, petals, stems, roots, bark, or even the whole plant. It is even possible for different oils to be extracted from one single tree or plant. For example, with the orange tree, the orange peel can be pressed for orange oil, the leaves and twigs distilled for petitgraine oil, and the orange blossoms for neroli oil. One tree can produce three different types of oils that are all very beneficial and therapeutic.

Today, about 200 different types of oils are being distilled, with several thousand chemical constituents and aromatic molecules being identified and registered. These aromatic substances and compounds within the oils will alter and change, based on weather conditions, climate, temperatures, and distillation factors. Today, 98 percent of essential oils are used in the perfume and cosmetic industry. In 1991, only 1/2 percent was used for Aromatherapy. In 1993, 2 1/2 percent were produced for Aromatherapy, or for therapeutic and medicinal application.

Essential oils have been recognized for their ability to decrease the viscosity of the blood, while increasing the velocity – thus **increasing cellular oxygen.** The greater the circulation of the blood, the greater the **oxygenation** of the tissues. Essential oils are recognized as being the greatest substances for **increasing cellular oxygen** through their normal function. When applied to the body by rubbing on the feet, essential oils will travel throughout the body and affect every cell, including the hair, within 20 minutes. They may have a lasting effect for as long as five months from only one application. This has been substantiated in the case of a cardiac patient who was tested before and after the use of oils for lowering blood pressure. The oils do not build up and store in the body because they are very subtle and volatile and have a high evaporation rate. Because of their chemical structure, they are metabolized like other nutrients in the cells.

One of the causes of disease, in both the plant and the human body, is the inability of nutrients to penetrate the cell wall. This causes cell deterioration, that leads to cell mutation – which in turn creates a host for bacteria and disease. One of the incredible aspects of essential oils is their ability to penetrate and carry nutrients through the cell wall to the cell nucleus.

The blood also carries the nutrients and oxygen needed to balance the potassium-sodium ratios within the cell, by penetrating the cell wall delivering those nutrients with the oxygen. **Oxygen** is the number one criterion in our environment for life and regeneration. Unfortunately, it has been compromised by our habits and environmental contamination.

Aromatherapy is a simple term used to cover a very broad and expanding field that we are just beginning to explore. I personally believe the knowledge being gained in the field may well have a great impact on the well-being of all mankind, as well as life on this planet as we know it. Aromatherapy means to treat with aroma through inhalation. The response to aroma has been proven to be as immediate as one to three seconds.

The integral part of the nose responsible for odor detection is the olfactory, consisting of two membranes. One of these is on each side of the mucous membrane covering the bony extension of the nose. The olfactory membranes are very tiny, and are well protected by the casing of the nose. They contain about 800 million nerve endings for processing and detecting odors. These receptors are so small that they are visible only through an electron microscope on high magnification. These nerve endings are triggered from a signal from the genes along the inside passage of the nose. The olfactory hair-like nerves receive the micro-fine, vaporized oil particles, carrying them along the axon of the nerve fibers, then connecting them with the synapse of the secondary neurons in the olfactory bulb. The nerve from the olfactory bulb extends back toward the mid-brain, which is a direct extension of the sense of smell, or limbic system, of the brain.

The impulses carried to the limbic system and the olfactory sensory center at the base of the brain, pass between the pituitary and pineal gland, and then to the amygdala – the memory center for fear and trauma. The impulses then travel to the gustatory center where the sensation of taste is perceived.

Only in 1989 was it discovered that the amygdala plays a major role in storing and releasing emotional trauma. And only odor or fragrance stimulation has a profound affect in triggering a response with this gland. Dr. Joseph Ledoux, of the New York Medical University, feels that this could be a major break-through in releasing emotional trauma.

It has been said that the limbic system (sense of smell) contains 10,000 to 100,000 times more information than sight, taste and touch combined. Perhaps this would explain why, when we are walking through a shopping mall and smell cinnamon rolls baking, we think of being in Grandma's house as a child.

The limbic system inside the brain is very unique in its function, and we find that foods are enjoyed more when the fragrance is experienced first. Moods are created and changed by various fragrances. Sexual energy is enhanced or decreased by certain odors. One area of great interest for someone who wants to be a good "Nose" is to understand that not all odor-particulants reach the olfactory. Odors must exist as a vapor or gas in order to affect olfactory sensory activity. This can happen through both the nasal or buccal cavities. Weather conditions, such as temperature and humidity, can all alter the odorous vapors or gases. For example, if you were to inhale orange oil during the dry heat of the desert, you would perceive little or no sensation of odor. However, by mixing the odorous vapors with moisture in the air, the fragrance becomes much more defined and recognizable.

There is a certain effect of turbulence generated by the airflow passing over the turbinates. This turbulence does not direct air upward to reach the olfactory gland, which is not located within the main airflow of the nose. People who have turbinate problems, such as a deviated septum, or pollups; or who have had nose surgery, may have a very

difficult time detecting the complete odor – simply because of the alter-
ing effect these problems may have had on the nerve programming and
sensory detectors. The same holds true for people who have worn a lot
of make-up, perfume and cologne, or who have used hair sprays, hair
colorings, perms and other products with synthetic odors.

Although many self-proclaimed aromatherapists claim they can really
identify the aromas, it is virtually impossible. What they smell are a few
sharp notes of the oil constituents. You find this very typical where
people live in polluted environments, such as in large cities like London,
Paris, Los Angeles, and New York. You also find it typical in farming
areas where there is continuous spraying of chemicals, pesticides, insec-
ticides, and fertilizers, and where there is heavy industrial pollution. I
am always amused when someone from these environments calls and
says, "The oils don't smell the same. Something must be wrong." They
are 100 percent right, but it isn't the oil that has the problem.

The olfactory gland is so interesting with its very receptive appetite
to the stimulation of odorous molecules. Many olfactory hairs respond to
only one kind of odor molecule, and simultaneously others will respond
to several different kinds of odors. This tells us that not all of the receptors are stimulated at the same time in the presence of odorous vapors.

The olfactory nerves are very much like other nerves and organs in
the body. They also respond to electrical signals and impulses that form
coded messages that are dispatched to various areas of the body. This
may be why some oil inhalation will increase endorphin, neuro-trans-
mitter and antibody production. When we realize that learning to identify oil molecules and categorize them by fragrance requires many years
of training, it is easy to understand why there are so few trained and
certified "Noses" in the world.

To train the nose is like developing a computer library by cataloging every odor intensity and density as well as the constituents of the oil. It is not a matter of having a good nose, or a sensitive one, but rather training the mind to focus and log all this information into olfactory memory. It is more difficult to establish olfactory memory, than it is with the senses of sight and sound. There are only 200 certified "Noses" in the world, and France employs 150 of them. This may help us to understand why it takes 20 years to become proficient as a "Nose."

Nose and Olfactory system

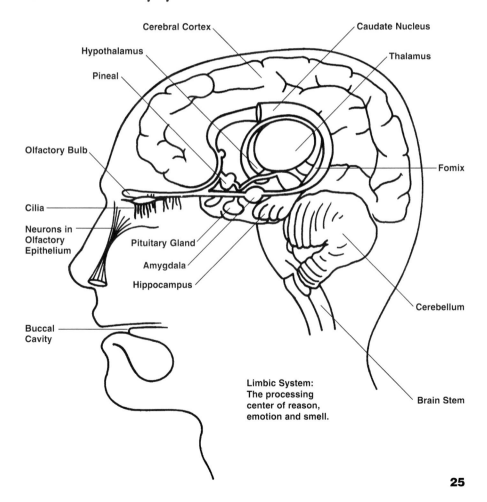

Fragrance is one of man's greatest enjoyments. Fragrance triggers memories of past experiences. The fragrance wafting through the air on a cool summer evening might remind us of a family outing in the park; or the smell of cinnamon rolls might remind us of the aroma we could smell while walking home from school. Fragrance creates a feeling of security, grounding and well-being.

How Do Essential Oils Work?
Oil Chemistry and Constituents

*E*ssential oils are chemically very heterogonic in their structure. This means they are very diverse in their effect and that they cause different actions unlike synthetic chemicals, which have basically one action. For example, lavender has been used for burns, insect bites, headaches, PMS, insomnia, stress, etc. Plants in nature are chemical factories. They take in the elements of the sun and earth, light and darkness, individually. They do this to receive the energy from both, thus converting them into molecules, carbohydrates, proteins and fats. These are the crude fuels which are broken down to produce ATP (adenosine triphosphate), which is a high octane fuel in the body.

Many scientific experiments have shown that essential oils can travel quickly when inhaled or applied through massage. The molecules of essential oils are so microscopic that they can easily penetrate the fatty layers of the skin. The liquid solubility of essential oils allows them to travel trans-cellularly, or directly through the cells. Their penetrating ability through the fatty tissue layers into the interstitial fluids may explain why essential oils enhance circulation, and why massage with oils can be so beneficial. The immune system can be greatly improved by increasing the velocity or movement of the blood, and by decreasing the viscosity or thickness of the blood. This improvement will enhance circulation, and is vital to good health as it affects the function of every cell and organ, including the brain.

Essential oils are made up of chemical groups and individual chemistry elements. Some of the primary elements responsible for the function of essential oils are **hydrogen, carbon and oxygen.** Most of the more obvious effects of essential oils can be attributed to such properties as **oxygen-containing molecules, sesquiterpenes, phenols, ketones, alcohols and aldehydes. Terpene alcohols,** for instance, are molecules comprised of 10 carbons, a number of hydrogens, and alcohol hydroxyl groups. This represents the different oxygen functional groups and their chemical symbols and names.

Oxygen, the key element in essential oils, plays an extremely important role along with other chemical elements, such as the phenylpropanes. Many of the aromatic constituents found in essential oils are derived from phenylpropanes. These are the precursors of amino acids, which link together to convert nutrients to proteins. These proteins, in turn, are the building blocks of the human body. Terpenols are another group of chemical constituents which are created from a single coenzyme A; and in which the human organism plays a crucial role in the production of vitamins, enzymes and the conversion to energy. Researchers have been astonished in how essential oils play a major role in their effect on blood circulation, not only in the **delivery of oxygen and nutrients to the tissues,** but also in assisting in the disposal of toxic waste from the tissues. The essential oil constituents found in various oils, like rosemary, peppermint, clove, cinnamon, melissa, oregano and thyme, have the ability to increase the production of ATP. These constituents also more efficiently **increase oxygen absorption within the cells and utilization of oxygen** from other sources, such as food and water.

Various constituents in essential oils have been adequately validated to increase the **oxygen** intake of the cells, as well as in their ability to utilize oxygen from other sources. Essential oils have many different chemical components in their various molecular structures. In fact, **there may be from 200 to 800 different chemical constituents within a single oil.** No two oils are alike in their affect on the body. Some constituents, such as **aldehydes,** are anti-infectious, sedative and calming to the nervous system. They are found predominantly in lavender and chamomile oils. **Eugenol** is antiseptic and stimulating, and is found in cinnamon and clove oil. **Ketones,** found in lavender, hyssop and patchouly oil, stimulate cell regeneration, liquefy mucous, and are helpful with dry asthma, colds and the flu. **Phenols** are antiseptic, and kill bacteria and viruses. They are found in oregano and thyme oil. **Sesquiterpenes,** which are predominant in frankincense and sandalwood, are anti-inflammatory, and work as liver and gland stimulants. They were found, in 1994, to go beyond the brain blood barrier, increasing oxygen around the pineal and pituitary glands. **Terpene alcohols,** found in juniper and citrus oils, are antibacterial, and work as diuretics and decongestants. (See reference section: Oil Constituents.)

Imagine how long the list would be if we were able to list all the constituents, as well as their major activities. Because of the incredible complexity and hundreds of different chemical constituents within one single oil, it becomes very clear that the value of essential oils is equally as immense – almost to the point of confounding the mind.

It is amazing when you think how certain chemical components in essential oils can destroy viruses and bacteria, while at the same time supply oxygen that delivers life-giving nutrients to the cell nucleus. In 1985, Dr. Jean C. Lapraz reported that **he couldn't find bacteria or**

viruses that could live in the presence of the essential oils of cinnamon or oregano. He found many other oils displaying the same qualities. This is very significant when we are faced with life-threatening viruses that are drug resistant. In our world today, we see incredible microbial mutations that are beginning to create a panic in many areas of the world. We should be more concerned about the *cause* of these mutations, rather than totally focusing on the virus. We sometimes get blinded by the sun's rays of today, while forgetting whether it was even shining yesterday.

In areas affected by the Chernobyl meltdown, there were numerous birth mutations in humans and animals, as well as in many varieties of plants. Now, 10 years later, we are still finding high levels of radioactive isotopes in the plant kingdom. It seems to be a well-established fact that radiation causes mutation. So, it stands to reason that if radiation can cause mutations in plants, humans and animals, it could possibly cause mutations in micro-organisms that are present in our own bodies. The problem becomes greater when we add the chemical pollutions from the air, water, food, manufacturing and processing plants, prescription drugs, social drugs, etc. Every form of synthetic chemical can cause mutation. With this possibility, we don't have to wait for the Ebola virus to travel from Africa. Because of our nutritional deficiencies and exposure to the drugs and chemicals, we continually have free radicals in our own bodies. These free radicals act as a host for disease, and weakens our immune system. Given enough time, we will have our own Ebola, or even worse. I really believe that in order to survive, we will have to change our lifestyles and return to the elements that God gave us.

I made an interesting discovery about skeletal alignment with a formula I made called **Valor.** I made the discovery while applying it to the bottom of a person's feet. **Valor** has a low frequency of 47 Hz, which works with the skeletal frequency of the bones. The bones have an electrical frequency of 45 Hz. These frequencies together allow the muscles and tendons to relax and the bones and vertebrae to move and self-correct the skeletal alignment. I know that sounds really "far out," but many people, even those with scoliosis, have received wonderful benefits from using the oils. It is a science that few understand, and most have a hard time comprehending – that is, until they have experienced it for themselves.

I always marvel at seeing pain diminish in seconds, without even touching the area that is damaged, or injured. Bone pain can be so excruciating and difficult to relieve. However, simple formulas like **Pane Away** and **Relieve It** have helped thousands of people find pain relief. **Pane Away** contains an oil called helichrysum, which has topical anesthesia-like action, and is a very powerful anti-inflammatory. **Relieve It** contains spruce, which carries the constituent methyl salicylate that works similar to cortisone. In just minutes, these two formulas will take away 75-90 percent of bone and tissue pain, and can be used singularly, or alternatingly.

The immune system is another important area we want to examine and understand. This is especially true with the tremendous weakness and continual degeneration caused by the chemicals we ingest, our polluted water and air, our denatured food, and our hectic lifestyles. I found a tremendous need in this area, and so I created an oil formula called **ImmuPower** to help give us some support and protection. This formula contains the oils of ravensara, oregano, thyme, mountain savory, clove, and black cumin, which are all antiviral and antifungal. Oregano, frankincense, clove and cistus are immune stimulators. Frankincense and clove are anti-tumoral and anti-cancerous. The action of the oils in this formula have all been documented by medical doctors and scientists in Europe, and then published in Dr. Pénoël's medical text on Aromatherapy. The following examples are from that textbook. Boswellia carterii is the botanical name for frankincense (page 328), and Origanum compactum is the botanical name for Oregano (page 383).

Boswellia carterii *Birdw.*
Encens ou oliban (oléorésine) Burséracées

Principes actifs
- Monoterpènes (40%) : (+)-α-pinène, (-)-limonène
- Sesquiterpènes: α-gurjunène, α-guaiène
- Alcools terp. : (+)-bornèol, trans-pinocarvèol ; farnèsol
- Composès bifonctionnels : -alcool-cètones olibanol, -alcool-oxydes : incensoloxyde

Propriétés
- Anticatarrhale, expectorante++
- Cicartrisante+
- Antitumorale (?), immunostimulante+++
- Antidépressive++

Indications (V.T.+++)
- Bronchites catarrhales et asthmatiformes; asthmes++
- Plaies, ulcères+
- Cancer (?), immunodéficience+++
- Dépression nerveuse++

Contre-indications: Aucune connue.

Origanum compactum *Benthum*
Origan à inflorescences compactes
(som. fl.) Lamiacées

Principes actifs
- Monoterpènes (25%): α et β-pinènes, myrcène, γ-terpinène, paracymène
- Sesquiterpènes (faible %) : β-caryophyllène
- Alcools non terp. : 1-octène-3-ol
- Monoterpènols (< 10%) : linalol, terpinène-1-ol-4, α-terpinèol
- Phénols monoterp. (60-70%) : carvacrol (major.), thymol
- Phénols méthyl-éthers : carvacrol M.E.
- Cétones monoterp. : camphre

Propriétés
- Anti-infectieuse puissante à zone d'action étendue (respiratoire, oro-intestinale, urogénitale, nerveuse, sanguine, lymphoganglionnaire) et à large spectre d'action (bactéricide+++, mycobactéricide+++, fongicide+++, viricide++, parasiticide+++)
- Tonique stimulante générale, immuno-stimulante

Indications (V.T.++++)
- Rhino-broncho-pneumopathies infectieuses+++
- Oropharyngites, entérocolites, dysenteries, amibiases+++
- Néphrites, cystites+++
- Névrites+
- Bactérémies, virémies, paludisme+++
- Adénites++
- Hypotension+
- Asthénies, fatigues nerveuses++

Contre-indications: Usage cutané, sauflocalisé (dermocaustique).

I was amazed with the effectiveness of **ImmuPower** when I had my own experience. Shortly after making this formula, I developed a serious throat infection after lecturing for three hours in a large air conditioned auditorium. I lectured without a microphone, then boarded an airplane and breathed its recirculated, contaminated air. I didn't pay any attention to my sore throat until two days later when I realized that it was getting worse, and I was running a fever over 103 degrees. My wife rubbed **ImmuPower** all over my throat and up my spine, and within 30 seconds the fever broke. At the same time, my throat opened, and I felt energy returning to my body. The next morning it was as though nothing had ever been wrong. I continue to marvel at the wonders of essential oils with every new experience.

Frequency of Essential Oils

*F*requency is defined as the measurable rate of electrical energy flow that is constant between any two points. Everything has an electrical frequency, and what an incredible discovery it was for me to learn that essential oils contain a frequency that is several times greater than the frequency of herbs and foods.

Robert O. Becker, M.D., author of the book, *The Body Electric,* validates the electrical frequency of the human body.

Richard Restick, M.D., one of the leading neurologists in Washington, D.C., and author of the book, *The Brain,* describes the electrical circuitry of the brain and body.

Royal Raymond Rife, M.D., developed a "frequency generator" in the early 1920s. With this he found that with certain frequencies he could destroy a cancer cell or a virus. He found that certain frequencies would prevent the development of disease, while others would destroy disease. Although Dr. Rife is no longer living, he left a legacy of incredible work in the field of electrical frequency, and its importance in the human body.

Nikola Tesla said that if we could eliminate certain outside frequencies that interfered in our bodies, we would have greater resistance toward disease.

Bjorn Nordenstrom, a radiologist of Stockholm, Sweden, wrote the book, *Biologically Closed Circuits*. He discovered in the early 1980s that by putting an electrode inside a tumor, then running a milliamp D.C. current through the electrode, he could dissolve the cancer tumor and stop its growth. He found that the human body had electro-positive and electronegative energy fields.

When we talk about frequency, we may become confused, knowing that light bulbs, TV, telephones, electric ranges, refrigerators, dishwashers, toasters, microwaves (heaven forbid), blenders, clocks, electric blankets, water beds, hair dryers, curling irons, computers, fax machines, etc., all have a frequency range of around 60 hertz. What we must realize is that there are different kinds of frequencies: incoherent and coherent, chaotic and harmonic, direct current (D.C.) and alternating current (A.C.). Electrical lights, appliances, and most man-made devices, have A.C. incoherent chaotic frequencies. Man, herbs, plant life, essential oils – those things created by God – operate with a D.C.-like current that has a coherent, harmonic frequency when healthy and in balance. It is like a grand piano that when tuned correctly has perfect harmonics and sound; but let one string be out of harmonic balance, and the sound becomes irritating and "sick."

For several years during my clinical practice, I researched the use of electrical energy for the purpose of reversing the disease process. I kept feeling that there had to be a more natural way of increasing a person's electrical frequency. This rationale led to the discovery of the electrical frequency of oils.

One of the things that I noticed with my patients was that they felt better emotionally when they first started to use essential oils. It seemed that just through simple inhalation of an oil, within seconds congestion would begin to loosen. Certain oils applied on location would decrease pain 50-80 percent within 1-3 minutes. Some even experienced a decrease in pain within seconds. I could not have thought that an oil applied to the bottom of the feet could travel to the neck and reduce pain by 70 percent within one minute. As I saw this happen again and again, I began to realize that there had to be other aspects and elements in the oils that had to be researched.

In 1992, the discovery was made that essential oils have a bio-electrical frequency measurable in hertz, megahertz and kilohertz, which was substantially higher than anything tested up to this time. Bruce Tainio of Tainio Technology, an independent division of Eastern State University in Cheny, Washington, was trying to find ways to clean up contaminated water and soil that had been destroyed by heavy chemical saturation. He had always been fascinated with energy, and set out to find a machine that would analyze the energies of the soil, water and plants. He finally decided that he would have to build this machine; and so with several other electrical engineers, he built the first frequency monitor in the world. He worked for four years, making alterations and perfecting it until it could be proven to be 100 percent accurate.

When Bruce Tainio and I began our conversations about frequency, Bruce offered to test the oils for their electrical frequency. I had tested the oils with other instruments and machines, but the results were not 100 percent accurate, and so were not accepted as a valid test. Bruce told me that the machine he had built was certified to be 100 percent accurate, and was being used in the agricultural field. That began the great discovery of the electrical frequency of essential oils, and was the first time in the world that the oils had been actually tested and documented.

Young Living and Tainio Technology were the joint discoverers of this great work. We determined that the average frequency of the human body during the day time is between 62-68 hertz (Hz). The brain frequency from 6:00 a.m. to 5:00 p.m. is between 72-78 Hz. Sometimes the frequency will be higher (even up to 90 Hz) with people who are studying for an exam, using their mind a lot, and those who are gifted with psychic abilities. Research has shown that if the frequency of the right and left brain lobes varied more than 3 Hz, a headache would begin. If the frequency varied more than 10 Hz, a substantial or migraine-type headache would develop. Understanding this, I created an oil formula containing such oils as helichrysum, chamomile and lavender, called **My-Grain.** Through simple inhalation of this formula, the Hz frequency in the head could be balanced and the headache reduced within a matter of seconds. With the oils of cardamom, rosemary, basil and peppermint, I created a formula called **Clarity** to help increase memory and mental accuracy.

The normal frequency range of the human body is between 62-68 Hz; but if it drops below that, the individual becomes a candidate for illness – simply because at this point the immune system will start to shut down. Cold symptoms appear at 58 Hz, flu symptoms at 57 Hz, candida at 55 Hz, epstein bar at 52 Hz, cancer at 42 Hz. There is much Hz research yet to do, but we are finding that these frequencies coincide 98 percent of the time with those we have already tested. Stated simply, if we can keep the body frequency high enough, and well oxygenated, we will be free of disease.

A. The frequency of a young man, age 26, while holding a cup of coffee, dropped in three seconds to 58 Hz. Without the use of oils, it took his body three days to go back up to normal.

B. Another young man, age 24, drank the coffee, and in three seconds his frequency dropped to 52 Hz. Inhaling the oil formula of **R.C.,** his frequency returned to normal in 21 seconds.

Example of Interaction of a Substance on the Body as Measured in Hertz

NORMAL RANGE OF HUMAN BODY 62 HZ TO 68 HZ

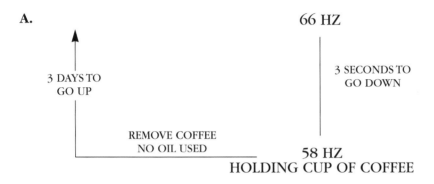

A.

66 HZ

3 DAYS TO
GO UP

3 SECONDS TO
GO DOWN

REMOVE COFFEE
NO OIL USED

58 HZ
HOLDING CUP OF COFFEE

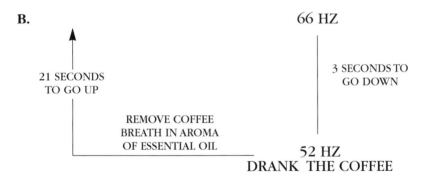

B.

66 HZ

21 SECONDS
TO GO UP

3 SECONDS TO
GO DOWN

REMOVE COFFEE
BREATH IN AROMA
OF ESSENTIAL OIL

52 HZ
DRANK THE COFFEE

Essential oils may not always prevent our frequencies from dropping, but they definitely assist the body in quickly re-establishing optimal frequency. This validates the statement that people using essential oils have a 60 percent greater resistance to illness. Not only that, but when using essential oils, they may recover 70 percent faster from a given illness.

Measuring in hertz, we found that processed/canned food had a zero Hz frequency, fresh produce had up to 15 Hz, dry herbs from 12-22 Hz, and fresh herbs from 20-27 Hz. Essential oils started at 52 Hz and went as high as 320 Hz, which is the frequency of rose oil. A healthy body, from head to foot, typically has a frequency ranging from 62 to 78 Hz, while disease begins at 58 Hz.

Clinical research shows that essential oils have the highest frequency of any natural substance known to man, creating an environment in which disease, bacteria, virus, fungus, etc., cannot live. I believe that the chemistry and frequencies of essential oils have the ability to help man maintain the optimal frequency to the extent that disease cannot exist.

The Ancient Art of Distillation and the Modern Technique of Adulteration

*T*he ancient art of distillation dates several hundred years before the time of Christ and to a large degree, still remains a mystery – simply because very little was written about the process. From the translation of the Ebers papyrus, we know that oils were extracted around 1500 B.C. In 1922, when King Tutenkhamon's tomb was opened, 350 liters of well-preserved oils were found in alabaster jars. Other more recent discoveries tell us that the Egyptian people were processing oils long before Tutenkhamon became king.

One very early method of oil extraction involved the use of goat fat and wool cloth. The aromatic substances were wrapped in goat fat and then rolled in a wool cloth. The wool cloth was then burned very slowly, allowing the oil to drop out of the plant material into the heated fat. Since the fat contained a large amount of water, and since oil and water are not soluble, when the fat cooled, it was pressed, thus separating out the oil.

Another common method of extraction was to fill a large stone tub with water, and allow the sun heat the water. The plant material containing the aromatic oil was masticated and placed in the hot water. As the oil separated from the plant material, it floated to the surface and was then skimmed off. This was also the period when floral water started to be used – over 4000 B.C.

Not long after this, people discovered that by heating the water and using steam heat for extraction, the oil production greatly increased. About this same time, it was also discovered that certain flowers, like jasmine, didn't produce oil when placed in the water. The reason for this was simple – the components of the oil were water soluble and would not separate from the water. The original method of using goat fat also didn't work because the goat fat was too dense for some of these delicate flower petals. This discovery encouraged more experimentation, which led to the discovery of using more refined goose fat. This method of extraction was later called *enfleurage* or "extraction with fat." More recently, lard was used, which eventually led to the development of chemical extraction that evolved in the late 1920s.

Steam distilling revolutionized the process of distilling, providing a more refined oil quality. Although there is much written about the use of oils, very little was recorded about the process of distilling the oils, perhaps due to lack of interest by the historians. Scriptorians were the record keepers in ancient times. The difference between ancient and modern writers was that the scriptorians did not travel from place to place writing about what they saw. They were not reporters; rather they were recorders of events, and so did not write in great detail. Oil processing was very commonplace, and in some areas was an everyday activity. However, the application and results of the oils were the topics they wrote about: ritual events, spiritual events and special healing experiences. One might make a comparison to the *Bible*. There is nothing recorded about the processing of frankincense oil, and yet its usage is talked about extensively. For example, much is written about Christ anointing with frankincense, and about various other healing events; yet we know nothing about how this oil was obtained. Building distillers and the processing of oils was not an event that created interest.

Today, however, we find ourselves trying to fit the pieces of the puzzle together by recreating the scenario of times, dates and places. From the records that have been found, we know now that the ancient people of Pakistan had a fairly refined distilling unit that was built with a condensing system. The Romans of 200 B.C. were famous for hot water bathhouses. The Israelites built steam bathhouses between 107-36 B.C., and may have been the first culture to develop a steam chamber that was separate from the chamber that held the plant material. There is no information, to my knowledge, that Egypt had a more refined distilling method than did the Israelites. This would lead me to believe that, although the Egyptians discovered and developed the uses of oils, the discovery and refinement of distilling techniques came from other countries and cultures.

As we study the ancient hieroglyphics in Egypt that depict expeditions to many countries, including India, we see that the Pharaohs exchanged Blue Lotus Oil with the king of India for slaves and other precious goods. Many of the writings and records of that day, however, were destroyed by Roman armies and other invading forces. Several millennia later, in July of 1798, Napoleon invaded Egypt, and was there exposed to the distillation of essential oils. It is believed that Napoleon could have been responsible for bringing some of the knowledge of steam-distillation from Egypt back to France.

For many years, an Arab named Avicenna, who lived about 1000 B.C., was credited with the discovery of the condenser. Research has proven this to not be true, however. In 1975, Dr. Paolo Rovesti, the director of the International Biocosmetic Research Center in Milan, Italy, led an archeological expedition to Pakistan. Upon studying the ancient writings in the museum of Taxila he found that there was a town situated at the foot of the Himalayas, dating back to 4000 B.C., that had a perfectly preserved distillation unit made of terra-cotta baked clay. This discovery led historians to consider an earlier time that the development of this extraction technology took place. They then realized that Avicenna was *not* the discoverer of cold-water condensing. To date, there is no evidence that the Egyptians discovered the refined method of cold-water condensing for distillation. Until 1974, the only written literature focusing on condensing was from Avicenna, in 1000 B.C. Therefore, he was credited with developing that process. However, it is also possible that the ancient Pakistan people learned about condensation from the Egyptians.

Taxila, Pakistan Distiller
Terra-Cotta Bake Clay Distiller, 4000 B.C.

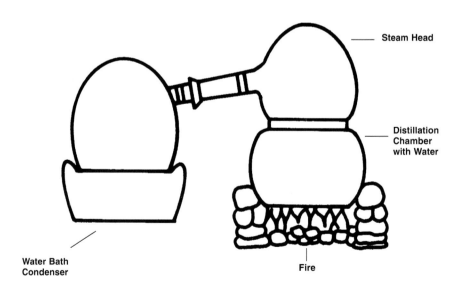

Steam Head

Distillation Chamber with Water

Water Bath Condenser

Fire

Cold Water Condenser

Very sophisticated Stone and Clay Distiller 103-36 B.C.
Believed to be built on orders of King Herod after the Egyptian Design.

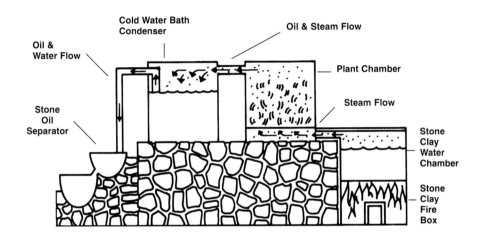

The plant materials high in aromatic oils, were placed in jars of water. These jars were then heated by the sun for oil extraction. Even during the reign of King Herod, just prior to the birth of Christ, the Egyptians were still using clay and stone jars for distilling. The ancient Israelites learned about distilling aromatic oils when they were slaves during their captivity under the reign of King Ramses. It is possible that they passed that information to the Jews after they returned to the promised land. About 36 B.C., the Israelites became masters at developing steam and steam bath houses patterned after the famous Roman bath houses. From what I discovered in 1994, while visiting the ruins of the ancient mountain-top ruins of the city of Masada that overlooks the Dead Sea, it is possible that during the time of Christ steam was discovered to have greater extraction ability than heated water. Masada may very well have been the location where steam-distillation began.

Picture of copper kettle and steam-distiller

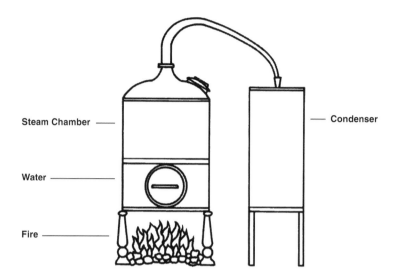

Most Americans do not have an ancestral, emotional, or psychological connection to essential oils. Products made with chemicals, such as perfumes, shampoos, makeup, deodorants, bath soaps, gels, salts, artificial car and home deodorizers and fragrances, as well as synthetic flavorings in food and beverages, have made it difficult for us to recognize a pure fragrance. For example, someone with a chemical allergy is already programmed for an allergic response to any fragrance associated with that substance. When the body is full of toxins, obnoxious gases are created in the blood and digestive tract, and a great deal of stress is placed on the sensory system. When the sensory system detects a fragrance, the mind automatically registers a similarity to that for which it has already developed an allergy. An immediate repulsive feeling and a sensitivity alert, goes out and says, "I can't tolerate this smell." In actuality, if the body is given a little time to adjust to the pure essential oil, it will not have a negative reaction.

Once in a while, individuals using an essential oil for the first time will say they broke out with a rash or had an allergic reaction. So many reactions are the body's chemical sensitivity kicking in and saying, "protect me." However, when I worked with people with severe allergies, even universal reactors, once they understood that pure essential oils actually detoxify and help re-establish cellular balance, they would calm down and realize they were not having a reaction. It's amazing to see how we in America have become sensitive to things around us, and yet at the same time we are desensitized to the things that are killing us, causing allergies, depressing the immune system, creating a weakness for diseases, such as candida, epstein bar, chronic fatigue syndrome, hypoglycemia, universal reactor symptoms, and other chemical sensitive problems. It just goes from level one to level six, manifesting different symptoms. Although doctors are diagnosing us with candida or allergies, this is really nothing more than an exaggerated condition of hypoglycemia going through its various stages of mutation.

As I was conducting research with a clinically controlled group, it was interesting to see that when people were treated for hypoglycemia, their candida symptoms went away. Their epstein bar virus also disappeared, and chronic fatigue, allergy and universal reactor symptoms all seemed to diminish substantially, and even disappear. Based on these findings, it was hard for me to believe that we really have all these diseases with which we are diagnosed. However, we must realize that germs and bacteria mutate as well as viruses mutate. This is why the same disease may manifest more than one symptom.

Because the sense of smell is so incredible, it is important to understand why we have these sensitivities and reactions. Let's go back to the early days of steam distillation, which is one of the most common ways of extracting oils from plants, trees, shrubs, flowers and herbs. This is accomplished by sending steam into a chamber that holds the raw product. As the steam rises, it stimulates the oil membranes in the plant. This causes the membranes to open, thereby releasing the oil molecule that has a micro-fine membrane around it, which is there to protect the oil. If the membrane is fractured while the oil is being released, the oil is damaged, and the molecular structure of the oil is altered. In nature, as the evening cools, the oil comes closer to the surface. As the day begins, the sun's warmth causes this membrane to relax, open and release the oil into the atmosphere. This is when we start to feel and smell a change in the air and why it is so incredible to walk in the garden or the forest in the early morning. It is so refreshing at sun up to feel the increased ozone and negative ions with the oxygenating molecules that have been released along with the intense fragrance.

When we consider releasing the oil so that it will retain its medicinal properties for the benefits we desire, we need to see how we can release the oil in a way similar to that of nature. Vertical steam-distillation gives us the greatest potential for protecting the oil and maintaining its integrity in order to protect its therapeutic benefits for fragrance and balancing the body. All of this must work on the areas in the brain that are connected to the limbic system, which affects emotional trauma release, appeases anxiety, and helps overcome depression. In ancient distillation, low pressure (5 lbs and under) and low temperature were extremely important in order to have the therapeutic benefits of this gentle process.

Marcel Espieu, who has been the President of the Lavender Growers Association for 21 years in southern France, told me when I was studying with him that the best quality of oil would be produced when the pressure was zero pounds during distillation. But because of the type of distillation that is used throughout France and other European countries, where wood-fired boilers are used, it is very difficult to control the pressure of the steam as it enters the chamber. In some chambers, the pressure will go up as high as 10 lbs. Marcel said, **"If you can build a distiller where you can deliver the steam into the chamber with zero pounds of pressure, you will have the finest oil."** I always remembered that statement as I was building different distillers and testing them to determine how to make them work better.

Over the past five years, I have also spent a great deal of time with Mr. Henri Viaud, learning the art of distillation. Both of these men say that low pressure and low temperature are an absolute must. Temperature has a very distinct effect on the oils. At certain temperatures, the oil fragrance, as well as the chemical constituents, can be changed. High pressures and high temperatures seem to cause a harshness in the oil where even the oil pH and the electro-positive and electro-negative balance are greatly affected.

It is important to understand that different trees, bushes, plants, flowers, and herbs require different amounts of time in the distilling chamber. For example, cypress requires 24 hours at a maximum of 245 degrees at 5 lbs pressure in order for all of the active constituents and properties to be released. But, if it is distilled for less than 22 hours, 18-20 of the primary constituents will be missing, which are absolutely essential to the therapeutic application of the oil and the expected response. However, most of the distilling operations throughout the world distill cypress for only one hour and 15 minutes. Although Spain is the largest producer of cypress oil in the world, I could not find one distillery in that country that would distill for the length of time required to produce quality. They absolutely refuse to distill for more that one and one-half hours. Mr. Espieu, who maintained the highest standard of cypress distillation, has now sold his operation because of increased government regulation and his inability to compete with the inferior and chemical distillation throughout Europe. However, I was fortunate to be able to contract with Mr. Espieu's cousin, who is presently distilling at the proper specifications in order to produce the highest quality for Young Living.

Lavender is distilled in France with a steam temperature of up to 350 degrees, and up to 155 lbs. of pressure for 15 minutes. Although the oil is easily sold and marketed, it is of very poor quality. The problem we have in America is that people are more concerned about price than quality. Naturally, you can sell lavender oil inexpensively if you can produce a pound of oil in 15 minutes, versus a pound of oil in an hour and a half. To maintain the highest grade of oil, and to be able to get all the properties in the oil that create that therapeutic effect in the healing of burns, reducing of headaches and fevers, overcoming insomnia and PMS, that oil must be of the highest grade and quality. Therefore, the lavender must be in the chamber for one and one half hours at no higher than 240 degrees F., and the pressure must be at zero pounds. Also, the size of the chamber or cooker, should not exceed 3500 liters in order to maintain the quality and integrity of the oil. There is also a hybrid lavender that produces lavendin oil. This hybrid has a high antiseptic property, and is great for sterilization; but it does *not* have as great a value in the Aromatherapy field. **In order to obtain quality oil, you must know the grower of the crop, how the crop is harvested, the time of harvest, the time of distillation, and who distills the oil.**

The flowering tops of the lavender produce the majority of the oil, and they should be harvested prior to the high heat of the day when they are in full bloom, just after opening. The oil is at the highest level just before the flowers completely open in the morning. The lavender needs to be cut and then left in the field during the heat of the day for two to three days. This increases the oil production and quality within the plant. The oil then needs to be distilled at low pressure and low temperature in the cooker for one and one half hours.

In the larger fields of the world during the distillation time, one can see chemical trucks hooked into the distillers pumping solvents into the water already in the boiler. This increases the oil production by as much as 18 percent, and then they can say, "Yes, it is steam distilled," and "No, we have not mixed chemicals with the oils, nor added propylene glycol to them." However, when you put a chemical in the water and force this with steam into the plant, it causes a fracturing of the molecular structure of the oil. This alters its fragrance and constituents because you cannot separate the chemicals from the oil after it comes through the condenser.

There are many devious things that some of the large oil producers are doing to promote and sell oils for a cheaper price. In America, we do not understand oil chemistry, nor how to test for oil quality. A Gas Chromatograph Mass Spectrophotometer (G.C.M.S.), which costs between $200,000 - $300,000, is a machine that tests the oils and determines their chemical constituents, percentages, and the range of activity that assures product quality. Throughout the world, there are a select few who are trained to smell. This individual is called a "Nose." It takes 21 years to become certified, and is one of the highest paid professions in the world. This individual can identify toxic constituents within an oil that have caused adulteration.

File: C:\CHEMPC\DATA\ETSAUGE.D
Operator: Dr JM Soulier
Date Acquired: 22 Sep 94   9:38 am
Method File: HEONCOL.M
Sample Name: Salvia sclarea
Misc Info: Gary Young 18/09/94   Sauge sclarée   USA
ALS vial: 1   n°2

CPG/SM : Hewlett Packard
Colonne : QUADREX 007 -1
3om x 0,18 mm x 0,25µln
Programme de T°C : 70°C : 7 min.
70 → 120°C : 2°C/min. 120 → 210°C : 2
Injecteur : split-less
Gaz vecteur : He
Volume H.E. injecté : 1 µl   210°C :

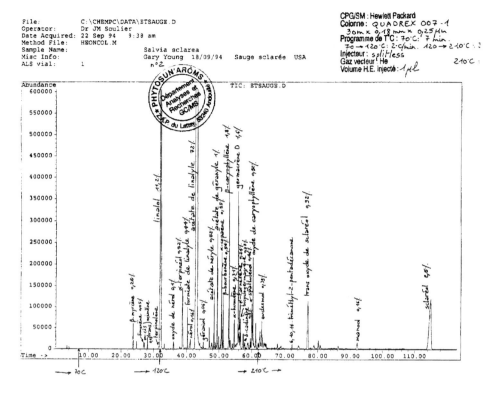

Most of the lavender oil sold in America today is lavendin, which is grown and distilled in either China or Russia. The oil production in both locations tests high in radio-active isotopes. They bring it into France, cut it with synthetic linolol acetate to improve the fragrance, add propylene glycol or SD 40, which is a solvent that has no smell and increases the volume, and then sell it in the United States as lavender oil. We in America don't know the difference, and are happy to buy and sell it for $5.00-7.00 a half ounce in health food stores, beauty salons, grocery and department stores, and through mail order. Frankincense is another example of an adultered oil. The frankincense resin or gum sold in Somalia costs between $30,000 and $35,000 per ton, and when steam distilled is very expensive. However, frankincense that is sold for as low as $25.00 per ounce, is distilled with alcohol. When these cut, synthetic and adulterated oils cause rashes, burns or other irritations, we wonder why we don't get the benefit we were expecting. We then come to the erroneous conclusion that essential oils don't have that much value. There are first, second, third and fourth stages of distillation, with each stage becoming weaker and weaker to which synthetic fragrance constituents are added and then sold to the unsuspecting public. Many people have jumped on the band wagon because of the money-making potential they see with essential oils. They buy cheap oils, rebottle them, label them as 100 percent pure essential oils, then market them without ever knowing their origin or who was responsible for the distillation.

Nestled high in a very remote area of the Rocky Mountains near St. Maries, Idaho, lies the beautiful Benewah Valley that is completely surrounded by mountains. Here lies the most beautiful ranch in the world, 12 miles from the closest town and one-half mile from the nearest neighbor. The six miles of dirt road have literally left this little spot of paradise undisturbed from the outside world. The ranch site was homesteaded in 1898 and used for cattle grazing in the summer months. In the winter months, the cattle were driven to the lower valley along the St. Joe and St. Maries River, for winter grazing. Prior to this time, the land was never really farmed, never had any chemicals added to it, and had not been plowed for 32 years.

When the frequency of the Benewah Valley was tested, it was discovered that there was a very special vortex of energy, even higher than that of Sedona, Arizona. The peace and tranquility of this valley is unsurpassed, and made the ideal location for the Young Living Farm. So, in 1992 I moved my growing project from Spokane, Washington, where I had started two years earlier. After seeing the number of essential oil producing farms

Young Living Essential Oil Farm 1994 – Lavender Field.

go out of business in France and Germany, I was concerned that the day would come when we would have a difficult time obtaining oils. Thus it was that in Spokane, in 1990 – and with merely one-half acre of ground – I started test planting to see what might grow and what oil could be produced. By 1992, it appeared that we had produced a sample of the finest lavender oil in the world. With this accomplishment, I felt I needed a special place to further this project. After many months of looking, I was led to the Benewah Valley. Currently, we have 50 acres in production.

In 1994, we produced an extremely high quality of peppermint and clary sage, as well as the first distilled wild tansy in the world. When we attended the essential oil medical convention in September of 1994, everyone who sampled the oils was excited and wanted to know where they could purchase some. They were fascinated with the wild tansy, since that was a new and almost exotic smell for them. Marcel Espieu, the former president of The Lavender Growers Association in France, whom I mentioned earlier, was thrilled with the fine quality of the oils, and was genuinely impressed that "this American" was really able to do it.

When we tested our oils in France, at the government laboratory of Phytosun'Arôm, they tested to show some of the highest levels of chemical constituents that had ever been recorded. These tests substantiated my feeling that we truly had produced the finest oil quality in the world. The Young Living Essential Oils Research Farm is the finest of its kind in North America. Young Living grows the plants, distills them for oils, manufactures the products, packages and distributes them and educates the consumer in the usage and benefits of essential oils.

The last time lavender was grown in the United States was in 1942, at Puget Sound. The project died, however, because of under-capitalization and lack of interest due to the growing excitement in Europe over the new craze of using chemical fragrance.

When I think back to our move from Spokane to the Benewah Valley, with just a few seeds and starts, to perhaps one of the cleanest and purest environments left in North America, I feel tremendous gratitude. At the same time, I am excited with what we have thus far accomplished, and I have great anticipation for what the future may hold. It is an awesome thought to consider that here in America we are rekindling and bringing back to life the ancient art of growing and distilling for the production of one of natures most precious gifts.

At the Young Living Research Farm, I built four different distillers; and, as I mentioned, the largest and only stainless steel vertical steam distiller in North America. I did this so we could control our operation in order to produce the highest quality oil possible. After building the first two distillers, I invented a steam decompression chamber and manifold that delivers the steam at zero pounds of pressure to the chambers.

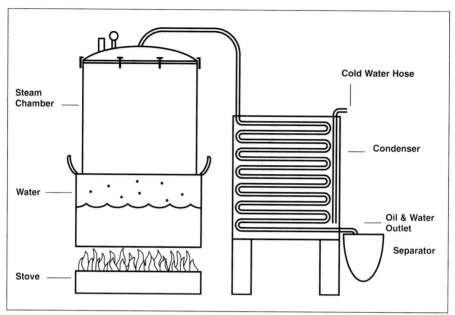

Steam Chamber

Cold Water Hose

Condenser

Water

Oil & Water Outlet

Separator

Stove

Gary's first distiller built at the Young Living Essential Oil Farm in 1991, St. Maries, Idaho.

Gary's third wood-fired distiller. Young Living Essential Oil Farm – August 1993, St. Maries, Idaho.

The first distiller was a very small model using a vegetable canner as the water reservoir and set on a gas stove. I then used a pressure cooker as the chamber for the plant material because the lid of the pressure cooker would seal and was equipped with temperature and pressure gauges. I drilled a hole, threaded it, and inserted another pipe for the steam discharge in the top of the lid beside the pressure gauge. Using a soft copper 5/8 inch pipe, I made a coil inside a five gallon bucket and placed a garden hose into the bottom of the bucket for adding cold water. This is a very simple unit to build. Remember, however, that the pressure cooker must be welded to the canner, and holes must be drilled in the bottom of the pressure cooker, in order to allow the steam to flow up through the plant material. I then installed an inline valve between the steam chamber and the condenser so I could increase the heat. With this unit, I could only produce about 1/16 of an ounce of

Young Living Essential Oil Farm, St. Maries, Idaho, Summer 1993 – Clary Sage.

lavender oil. It was a lot of fun and very exciting to get that 1/16 ounce of oil!

The second model was 50 liters larger, enabling me to produce up to one ounce of oil per load. Even so, the steam volume could not be controlled with this application.

The third distiller I built was 150 liter, wood-fired, portable distiller that we could use out in the woods for testing. I invented my own special design that enabled me to produce the highest quality of oil in the world. In the summer of 1994, with the help of Ted Jacobs, a metallurgical engineer, I built the large distiller we now use. This distiller is powered with two independent diesel-fueled boilers. One is 100 Hp and the other is 25 Hp. Both chambers are built of stainless steel, and one holds 2,271 liters, while the other holds 3,550 liters. With the steam chamber standing upright, or vertical, the steam is able to rise gradually without pressure penetrating the plant material. One of the secrets of distilling is to have little or no pressure with large steam volume to flood the chamber.

From my evaluation of the previous distillers I had built, and working with Marcel Espieu and Henri Viaud in France, I learned that dry steam helped prevent hydrolysis that causes a loss of oil production and certain water soluble constituents. Because of this problem, I designed a steam dryer and decompression chamber through which the steam could flow before entering the chamber. From there, I built a manifold system into which the steam could flow without pressure under the chamber. I specifically designed four jets on the manifold to allow the steam to flow directly into the chamber. The design of the jets causes the steam to spin in a clockwise direction, creating a vortex. I found this gives a greater and more even distribution of the steam to the plant material.

There are many factors to consider in order to produce quality oil, such as the weather conditions, soil conditions, maturity of the plant, and the time of day of harvest. When should the plant be cut? Before bloom, during bloom, post bloom, or during seed development? Should the plant be cut with dew on it, or after the dew is gone? Should the plant be cut during the heat of the day, or during the cooling of the evening? After the plants are mature, how many days of heat should they experience before they are cut? Then, after the plant is cut, should it be distilled immediately, or should it lay in the fields and cure for a few days? The size of the distilling chamber is crucial to producing quality oil. The temperature of the pre-heating chamber, and the length of time that the steam is in the chamber with the plant material, is extremely important as well. Is there a time of the day that is better than another for distilling? The condenser is important in cooling the water, as well as the water discharge and over-flow.

There are also many possible dangers and risks in working with steam, compression and the possibility of vapor lock. In most states you have to be a certified boiler operator. Then there is the cost. I built my distiller, myself, with donated labor. My material cost was about $26,000 for one chamber, and $5,000 to $6,000 for the 25 Hp boiler. A 100 Hp used boiler costs about $15,000 - $20,000, and building with stainless steel, as I did, costs even more. To have a distiller the size I built would cost $100,000 to $125,000. Presently in the U.S. there are only one or two manufacturers building distillers for the food flavoring industry using such oils as peppermint and spearmint. These distillers are manufactured out of aluminum, and are built horizontally for high pressure and temperature. The one and only manufacturer of low-pressure and low- temperature distillers, in Lyons, France, closed down and went out

Young Living Essential Oil Farm. First vertical stainless steel distiller built in America. Designed and built by Gary Young, with the assistance of Ted Jacobs and Jack L. L. Young. St. Maries, Idaho, August 1994.

Young Living Essential Oil Farm. First firing of new distiller after construction. Gary Young - Left, Jack L. L. Young - Right. St. Maries, Idaho, August 1994.

of business in 1992. As you can see, plant distilling is not something to entertain as a hobby.

We were very specific in choosing land that had never had chemicals on it. All the growing and distillation production on our farms in Idaho, Utah, and France are strictly organic. We begin with the pure seeds and take them all the way through the growing, harvesting, distilling, formulating, packaging and marketing. I travel around the world to see the farms and the distillation to insure organic production for the purest and highest quality of the oils. This way we know what we have and can stand behind the production and the quality.

There are many people in America who, after a weekend course, call themselves "Aromatherapists." They know absolutely nothing about oil chemistry and the very specific ways in which oils need to be formulated in order to maintain a harmonic synergistic action in oil formulations and products. As a result, we have people who take a class or listen to a lecture and say, "Oh, there's nothing to this." Then they purchase oils, mix them, and create their own blends. This is fine if it is only for fragrance and perfume; but when making oil formulas for a specific therapeutic need, you can alter and change the chemistry action and totally neutralize the effect you are desiring if you don't understand the chemistry. This is another reason I spent 10 years in Europe studying in the universities, laboratories, hospitals, museums and libraries. I traveled to distilleries, farms, and essential oil companies – any place where I could do research in my desire to have as much knowledge as possible in my quest to help bring this ancient science back to the world. My research is never-ending, as I continue to search all over the world for ways to produce the finest and highest quality of oils possible.

Young Living Essential Oil Farm, Summer 1994 – Clary Sage – just before harvesting.

Young Living Essential Oil Farm, Summer 1994 – Peppermint – ready to harvest.

Many books sold on essential oils are of grave concern, especially since several European writers have discovered a new market potential in the United States. As I have studied in Germany, Austria, Spain, Switzerland, Italy, France, England, Israel, and Egypt, where production is taking place, I have found that people there who are working in essential oils have not taken the time to write and publish books. The journalists who write the books are not the ones doing the research. Many of the books sold in America have little validity in the things they say and the claims they make. I emplore you to read them with caution and with an open mind, with the understanding that a lot of what you read is not valid or true. One popular book in America is written by a woman claiming to be a medical doctor. However, she purchased her degree in Sri Lanka for $1,000, and most of her material has been plagiarized from doctors and researchers involved in this great work. I do, however, recommend books written by authors such as Jean Valnet, M.D., Marguerite Maury, Daniele Ryman, Shirley Price, and Robert Tisserand.

I was one of the first in North America to conduct clinical research using essential oils for the treatment of degenerative disease. I have also spent many years and tens of thousands of dollars learning how to put essential oils into food supplementation. Because of the properties of essential oils, it seemed obvious to me that the oils acting as a catalyst would help increase the delivery of the nutrients through the cell wall into the cell nucleus for greater absorption and metabolic effects. My research has been extensive; and in the last few years, I have spent more time traveling than being at home, which has made it impossible for me to do much writing. I have been compiling information for years, and the research that I have conducted for the past 11 years I hope to have included in a more extensive book in the near future.

Young Living Distributor Tour to France, May 1992.

Young Living Distributors weeding at the Young Living Farm in southern France, May 1992.

The Uses, Misuses and Applications of Essential Oils

*I*n the world of Aromatherapy, many opinions are expressed on how to use essential oils. From the many books that I have read, and from my travels and research, I have not seen anyone who has used essential oils, or tested them, in as many applications as I have.

In 1991 for example, the oil of helichrysum was virtually unknown to the world and had only very limited use as an anti-inflammatory, antibacterial agent, and as a perfume fixative. Because it is an expensive oil, and there are many other less expensive oils with these same properties, helichrysum has not been studied. At that time, there were approximately 28 pounds of helichrysum produced in three countries of the world: Corsica (producing the best quality), Italy and Yugoslavia.

In the summer of 1991, my son slammed the car door on his finger, splitting it wide open. At that time, I was working in my lab analyzing helichrysum. Knowing that it was antibacterial, I put it on the open wound before I prepared a basin of warm water to clean his finger. Within a minute after applying the oil, he stopped crying and announced that his finger didn't hurt. This is how I discovered that helichrysum had topical anesthesia-like activity. This experience led to the formulation of **Pane Away.** As of this writing, Young Living purchases and distributes 98 percent of all the helichrysum produced in the world today. In 1995, we purchased the entire crop of helichrysum from Corsica.

It is important to keep in mind that many areas of essential oils have not as yet been studied – particularly the area of application. In 1992, I discovered that some hearing conditions could be improved with the application of essential oils; and at the present time, three people who were born deaf have experienced as much as 40 percent restoration of hearing. We have also seen 100 percent restoration of hearing loss, from accidents, through the use of essential oils.

In January of 1992, I discovered that the formula **Valor** could help the spine self-correct a misalignment. Another formula helped improve eye conditions. In 1991, it was discovered that frankincense, when combined with myrrh, sage and black cumin, could help reduce breast tumors. There are now seven documented cases in which the elevated P.S.A. count returned to normal after using this same formula. This does not mean, however, that the oils cured anything! My second book will go into detail and explain how this works scientifically.

Many writers and self-proclaimed Aromatherapists assert that oils cannot be used *neet* (meaning straight, without a carrier oil, or undiluted). I have been applying oils in therapy for over 12 years, and rarely do I dilute them unless doing a full body massage. Most of the oils sold in the United States are adulterated in one form or another. Therefore, it is safer to dilute oils that are not from Young Living. Even though your supplier may claim to purchase oils from a credible source in Europe, most European suppliers sell three to four different grades of oils. Unless you are buying more than $30,000 worth of oils a month, you cannot afford to purchase the Grade A quality oils; so based on your monthly purchase your supplier will prequalify you for what grade they will sell to you. In addition to the oils that we produce, Young Living purchases tens of thousands of dollars in oil volume per month. By 1997, with our current growth rate, we will be purchasing over one million dollars in oil volume yearly.

It is important to remember that many oils smell similar to the untrained "nose," and only through a G.C.M.S. (Gas Chromatograph Mass Spectrophotometer) can you really identify the inferior quality oils.

In April of 1995, Young Living established a working agreement to conduct joint-research with the chemistry and biochemistry departments at Weber State University in Ogden, Utah. There we are presently conducting a comparative quality analysis on the Young Living Oils, as well as on the oils of other companies. With these comparisons, we can better understand the caution needed when buying oils as they become available from so many different places.

There are many beneficial ways of using the oils besides massage and diffusing. I have used and taught several applications that I have found to be quite valuable. Most oils may be worn as a perfume or aftershave. The fragrance usually determines if you would wear them this way. The oils may be applied just about anywhere on the body that you desire – your neck, face, wrists, over heart, arms, hands, feet, etc. A few oils, such as cinnamon or the formula of Thieves, are high in phenols, and may be a little too hot to apply *neet,* or directly on the skin. In this case, one should apply these oils to the bottom of the feet, or dilute them with the **V-6 Mixing Oil,** or a pure vegetable oil.

When applying the oils to the skin, it is not necessary to wait between the application of different oils. You would wait only if you were doing an experiment and wanted to see if there was a difference in feeling or result from one oil to the next, and if you are just becoming acquainted with the oils. Oils have the ability to help detoxify the cells and blood of the body. Too many oils applied at the same time could cause you to detoxify too quickly. This is not harmful, but may be a little unpleasant; so proceed slowly until you learn how your body is going to respond. In normal application, simply layer one oil on top of the previous oil.

Vita Flex Therapy

Vita Flex Therapy means "vitality through the reflexes." With Vita Flex, the oils are applied on the contact points of the body. The healing energy is released through the electrical impulses by the contact between the fingertips and the reflex points. This stimulates an electrical charge that follows the neuro pathways of the nervous system to where there is a break in the electrical circuit. The break in the electrical circuit will be directly related to an energy block caused by toxins, damaged tissues, or loss of oxygen. This reflex system of controls encompasses the entire body and mind, releasing all kinds of tension, congestion and imbalances. This technique was believed to have originated in Tibet many thousands of years ago, long before acupuncture was ever discovered. With Vita Flex, the weakened or injured areas are corrected on the electrical reflex points, thus preventing further injury. This results in less stress, which allows for quicker and more efficient healing.

To use the Vita Flex Therapy, always place the oils in the palm of your hand. Then use your dominant hand to stir the oils clockwise three times before applying them on location. The same thing applies for those who practice reflexology, acupressure, spinal touch, zone therapy, etc. All types of therapies will result in a significant improvement when combined with the oxygen and high electrical frequency of the oils.

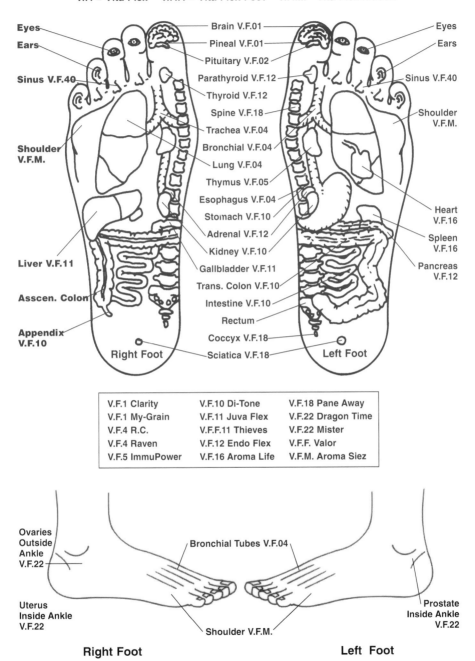

V.F. = Vita Flex   V.F.F. = Vita Flex Feet   V.F.M. - Vita Flex Muscle

Eyes
Ears
Sinus V.F.40
Shoulder V.F.M.
Liver V.F.11
Asscen. Colon
Appendix V.F.10

Brain V.F.01
Pineal V.F.01
Pituitary V.F.02
Parathyroid V.F.12
Thyroid V.F.12
Spine V.F.18
Trachea V.F.04
Bronchial V.F.04
Lung V.F.04
Thymus V.F.05
Esophagus V.F.04
Stomach V.F.10
Adrenal V.F.12
Kidney V.F.10
Gallbladder V.F.11
Trans. Colon V.F.10
Intestine V.F.10
Rectum
Coccyx V.F.18
Sciatica V.F.18

Eyes
Ears
Sinus V.F.40
Shoulder V.F.M.
Heart V.F.16
Spleen V.F.16
Pancreas V.F.12

Right Foot   Left Foot

V.F.1 Clarity	V.F.10 Di-Tone	V.F.18 Pane Away
V.F.1 My-Grain	V.F.11 Juva Flex	V.F.22 Dragon Time
V.F.4 R.C.	V.F.F.11 Thieves	V.F.22 Mister
V.F.4 Raven	V.F.12 Endo Flex	V.F.F. Valor
V.F.5 ImmuPower	V.F.16 Aroma Life	V.F.M. Aroma Siez

Ovaries Outside Ankle V.F.22
Uterus Inside Ankle V.F.22

Bronchial Tubes V.F.04

Shoulder V.F.M.

Prostate Inside Ankle V.F.22

Right Foot   **Left Foot**

When using the Vita Flex Technique with essential oils, it is best to start on the bottom of the feet. The foot charts I have created may seem a little different from the standard reflexology charts. I found that while testing the electrical currents with the frequency monitor, the contact points were a little different than those shown on standard foot charts. The Vita Flex charts are based on electrical frequency tracing, which is much more accurate.

For those using oils for the first time, the V.F. numbers on the labels of the oil Blends correspond to the location on the feet, and are marked and numbered on the foot charts. This way you can determine where to apply the individual Blends on the bottom of your feet. If you are not familiar with the Vita Flex Technique, you can order the "Science and Application" video, which demonstrates this application as well as the Rain Drop Therapy.

Acupuncture

There are two methods of applying oils. The point of the needle can be dipped in the oil and then inserted, or the needle may be rolled in the oil and then inserted. The antibacterial properties of the oils will sterilize the needle. When using the laser acupuncture technique, apply the oil to the contact point and then use the laser.

Colonics

Oils are not water soluble, and will float to the top; so they must be emulsified with a product like lecithin, milk, glycerin, alcohol, disper (a natural emulsion made from all natural ingredients with lecithin), vegetable oil, etc. However, it is not very practical for every-day application. The best technique is to mix 10 to15 drops of the essential oils with one tablespoon of the **V-6 Mixing Oil,** and then insert the solution like an enema, using an ear bulb syringe, and retain through the night.

Sitz Baths

Add 5-15 drops of the essential oils (or as desired) to one gallon of warm water, then keep the water agitated. This is excellent therapy for hemorrhoids, candida, aching muscles, after birthing discomfort, etc.

Compresses

Fill the basin with two quarts of hot water and add the essential oils of your choice. Stir vigorously and then lay a face cloth or hand towel on top of the water. After it is completely saturated, wring out the water, place the cloth over the area, then cover the wet towel with a heavier dry towel for a longer lasting effect. Place a hot water bottle, or heating pad, over the top of the dry towel and cover it with a third dry towel for one to two hours.

Inhalation and Diffusing

This is one of the most pleasant and effective ways of using essential oils. The Young Living aromatic diffuser is the easiest and simplest way of putting the oils into the air for inhalation. The diffuser disperses the essential oils into a micro-mist that remains suspended for several hours – effectively reducing bacteria, fungus and mold, while freshening the air with natural fragrances. Diffusing releases oxygenating molecules, antiviral, antibacterial and antiseptic properties, as well as negative ions that kill bacteria. When diffused, essential oils have been found to reduce air-born chemicals, bacteria and metallics in the air, as well as to help create greater spiritual, physical and emotional harmony.

The oils may be diffused at various times throughout the day, as desired. However, they are best diffused for 15 to 30 minutes as you become accustomed to them. As you learn how oils work, you may choose to diffuse them for a longer period of time. You may also diffuse different oils one after another. You may mix single oils or a single oil and a blend, but do not mix the blends as that will not only change the frequency and the desired results for which they were created but also the fragrance.

The Young Living diffuser is an air-operated jet chamber similar to a carburetor. The air-pump creates a pressure that disperses the oil through a jet into a glass nebulizer (tube). This reduces the oil into a fine micro-mist vapor that, within seconds, covers approximately 2,500 square feet, creating the most ideal purification system available. Place the diffuser in the central part of the house in an elevated place, such as on the mantel or on a high bookcase shelf. A circulating fan will help move the oil mist through the air more quickly.

You can also use a tissue, cotton ball, handkerchief, towel, etc., in hotel air vents, car vents, or even the vents at home or work. The oils are terrific on the sheets and pillowcases, as well. It's a marvelous experience sleeping with a little **Dream Catcher** on your pillow. Oils can also be put in vaporizers and humidifiers. These all have great value. However, it is important to remember that heat will reduce some of the benefit.

Earaches

Put one drop of **helichrysum** on a cotton ball, and place the cotton ball in the ear for any kind of an earache.

Baths and Showers

Add the oils to the bath water while the tub is filling. The oils will separate when the water calms down. As you step into the tub, your skin will draw the oil quickly from the top of the water, so choose gentle oils like **lavender, rosewood, chamomile, sage, ylang ylang,** etc. The greatest benefit will be derived from using the **Bath and Shower Gel Base,** then making your own formula. Add 15 drops of your favorite essential oil to one-half ounce of **Bath and Shower Gel Base.** Then add this to the water while the tub is filling. When showering, add the oils to the face cloth or lufa sponge. **Evening Peace, Relaxation** and **Sensation Bath and Shower Gels** are wonderfully soothing in the evening. **Morning Start** is a terrific way to jump-start your day.

Dishwater, Clothes Washers and Dryers

Adding oils can increase the antibacterial benefits, providing greater hygiene, and make your clothes come out with a refreshing, clean smell. A couple of drops of **Melrose** or **lemon** in the dishwater make for sparkling dishes and a great-smelling kitchen.

Water Purification Systems

Add 3-5 drops of your favorite oil to the post-filter on your water purification system. Putting the oils on the filters of your unit helps to increase the oxygen in the water as well as to increase the frequency, making the water more energizing to drink for both children and adults. You can have fun changing the taste of the water by putting different oils on the filters, such as **peppermint, lemon, birch,** and **cinnamon.**

Cleaning and Disinfecting

Lemon, spruce or **fir** oil work well for polishing furniture and cleaning and disinfecting bathrooms and kitchens. Put a few drops on your dust cloth or put 10 drops into water in a spray bottle, then spray it as a mist. **Lemon** oil is terrific for dissolving gum and grease, and the **Purification Blend** is fantastic for removing mold and fungus.

Painting

Add one 15 ml. bottle of your favorite blend of oil to any five gallon bucket of paint. Stir vigorously, mixing well, and then either spray paint or paint by hand. When I did this in our office, we were all amazed that not only were there no paint fumes, or after-smell, but we enjoyed the wonderful smells of **Purification, White Angelica** and **Abundance** for weeks after I finished painting. I tried a different blend in each new five gallon bucket.

Raindrop Therapy

The Raindrop Therapy is a method of using Vita Flex, reflexology, massage techniques, etc., and essential oils applied on various locations of the body to bring it into structural and electrical alignment. It has typically been used to help straighten spinal curvatures and to fight against viruses. It has been discovered that many viruses lie dormant along the spine, including the virus that causes scoliosis. The Raindrop therapy is a mild and non-intrusive application of a combination of several techniques that have proven to be effective from a small degree, to what would appear to be miraculous. I have never seen it fail, and have been surprised by many unexpected and fruitful results. Of course, this cannot be taken to mean that it will always work.

Raindrop Therapy is designed to bring balance to the body with its relaxing and mild application. It will help align the energy centers of the body, and release them if blocked – all without using hard pressure and trying to force the body, which should never be done.

The Raindrop Therapy application is most often used as a foundation to set the stage for any number of therapeutic applications; for example, a full body massage.

Raindrop Therapy is a simple application of dropping the oils like little drops of rain from about six inches above the body. Hence, the name, Raindrop Therapy. It takes approximately 40 minutes to complete. The oils will continue to work in the body for about 5 to 7 days after the treatment, with continued re-alignment taking place during this time. I have never seen the treatment hurt, and it has always been beneficial.

The Raindrop Therapy is best done using a massage table with the person receiving the treatment lying down. It may also be given with the individual sitting in a chair or lying on the floor. I have found that the intent of the individual receiving and applying the therapy is helpful. The essential oils, because they are derived from plants and are the very life force of the plant, carry an intelligence and a frequency. When you combine the electrical frequency and the intelligence of both the body and the oil, a greater healing process begins. Deepak Chopra, M.D., in his book *Quantum Healing,* describes in detail the working of intelligence in the human body. I firmly believe that if you give the body the proper tools with which to work, it is capable of healing itself.

The Raindrop Therapy is not a "cure all," nor a magic bullet. A healthy body is the result of a well-rounded program of exercise and proper diet. Health is everything you do, say, hear, see and eat. The Raindrop Therapy is a powerful tool to use to help restore a balance of good health.

Although this therapy is explained as simply as possible, I would strongly suggest that you watch the **"Science and Application"** video from Young Living so you can see this technique demonstrated. After watching the video, with the explanation given here, it will be even easier to use this technique.

The following oils will be needed and should be used in this order:

1. **Valor** works on the electrical and energy alignment of the body. The key to using this blend of oils is patience. Once the frequencies begin to balance in these areas, a structural alignment can then occur. **This is the most important oil that we use in this application.**

2. **Thyme** has been scientifically proven to be anti-infectious, anti-bacterial, and antiviral. There is some indication that scoliosis is the result of some viral and/or bacterial activity that has taken place in the body at some point before the scoliosis began. The essential oil can easily penetrate the body, and may help kill any virus or bacteria that may be present.

3. **Oregano** works similar to thyme, but is more aggressive, and may help stimulate the immune system, balance the metabolism, and strengthen the vital centers of the body.

4. **Birch** is anti-inflammatory and may help to relieve pain. It is excellent for bone as its primary chemical constituent, methyl salicylate, has a cortisone-like activity, which may help with arthritis, tendonitis and rheumatism.

5. **Cypress** may help circulation, and may help relieve spasms, cramps, edema, cellulite, varicose veins and water retention.

6. **Peppermint** is used to soothe and strengthen the nerves. It also helps bring harmony between the other oils in order to enhance their individual activity.

7. **Basil** smooths the muscles with its antispasmodic activity and is also known to stimulate the nerves, alleviate mental fatigue, and relieve migraine headaches.

8. **Marjoram** is antispasmodic, and may help relax the muscles and relieve cramping, aches and pains.

9. **Aroma Siez** works similar to **marjoram;** but because it is a blend of oils that have many similar properties, it is a great complement to marjoram and will enhance the results.

10. **V-6 Mixing Oil** is used to dilute the oils that are high in phenols, which may give the skin a burning sensation for people with fair to light skin, like red-heads and blondes. After applying **oregano** and **thyme,** it is best to use 10-15 drops of the **V-6 Mixing Oil** over the areas where these oils have been used.

11. **Ortho Ease Massage Oil** is to be applied over the entire area after you have finished with the Raindrop application. **Ortho Ease** has been reported to be beneficial for stress, muscle cramps, arthritic pain and tension.

The Raindrop Technique

Preparation: Have the person lie face down on the table with the head resting in the face cradle of the massage table, or with the head slightly lower than the rest of the body. The body should be as straight as possible with the hips flat on the table. The arms can be resting along side the body, or over the edge of the table.

You will need three medium-size towels, hot water, and a way to protect the modesty of the individual since he or she will be moving around.

Step 1

Place six drops of **Valor** on each foot. It works best if there are two people who can apply the **Valor.** One person can apply six drops on each shoulder, and the other person can apply six drops on each foot. The person who is at the feet may sit or kneel with the right hand holding the right foot and the left hand holding the left foot. The palm of the hand should be flat against the bottom of the feet, with as much hand to foot contact as possible.

The individual assisting is at the head sitting or standing with right hand to right shoulder and left hand to left shoulder, with as much hand to shoulder contact as possible. Now you must just be patient. Do not attempt to force your thoughts or make something happen. Let your mind be free and peaceful. You may feel an energy flowing through the person receiving the treatment up through the hands and arms of the individual applying the oils. The receiver may feel a mild heat on the feet, or a tingling sensation around the feet, or an energy working up through the legs to the back, even as high as the head. With some individuals, the giver may feel the hands become cold. If this happens, just hold on and do not break contact with the individual, even though you may want to, as it interrupts the procedure.

This procedure is the foundation for everything that follows. In most cases, you will see some realignment of the spine. I have watched the vertebrae move under the skin with just this small amount of application. The hands will usually be held to the feet and shoulders for 5 to 10 minutes. As you gain experience with the application, you will get a sense for how long to hold the feet and shoulders. If you are working by yourself, the application works well just holding the feet, which is the most important.

The results will depend largely upon the frequency of the person holding the feet. If there are other people in the room with negative attitudes, and if the individual applying the oils does not have a high enough frequency to block out that negative interference, the results may be less than optimal.

Step 2

Next comes the application of the oils of **thyme** and **oregano.** Hold the bottle approximately six inches above the skin and let five drops of each oil drop from the bottle evenly spaced along the spine from bottom to top (sacrum to atlas or 1st cervical). Try to stay in the electrical field as much as possible. It does not matter which oil is applied first. Apply one oil, then layer it in by gently spreading it evenly along the curvature of the spine. Apply the second oil the same way. You don't need large drops, and more is not better. Then apply 10 to 15 drops of the **V-6 Mixing Oil** to prevent any discomfort.

With four inch-strokes in a brushing motion, and using the nail side of your finger tips, lightly feather up the spine from the sacrum to the atlas. Remember to follow the curvature of the spine. Repeat this technique two more times, always starting at the sacrum.

Now, use your finger tips again, starting at the sacrum, feathering up again about four inches, and then flaring your finger tips out to the side of the body. The right hand will move to the right, and the left hand will move out to the left. Begin your stroking again, starting at the sacrum, stroking up about eight inches, and then flaring out again. Begin your stroking again, starting at the sacrum, feathering up about 12 inches, and then flaring the fingers out. Continue this technique to the atlas and flare out through the shoulders. Repeat this whole sequence two more times.

The final move in this step is to start at the sacrum, and in full-length strokes, feather all the way up the spine to the atlas. Then feather your finger tips out over the shoulders, and repeat two more times.

Step 3

Now apply the oils of **cypress, birch, basil,** and **peppermint** in that order. Apply four or five drops of the first oil along the length of the spine. Layer it in by evenly spreading it with your finger tips. Then do the same with the other three. Starting on one side of the spine, gently massage the oils in along the spine. **Do not work directly on the spine. Do not force it or apply direct pressure.** Start at the sacrum and use the finger tips of both hands placed side by side. Then, in a circular clockwise motion, work up the side of the spine to the atlas, pushing or pulling the tissue in the direction you want the spine to move. This technique helps to create a "space" for the spine to move. After finishing one side of the spine, walk around to the other side of the individual and begin on the second side, starting from the sacrum and working up to the atlas. Repeat this procedure two more times.

Next, using the index and middle fingers of either hand, place the fingers so that they "straddle" the spine beginning at the atlas. In this position, you move from top to bottom. With mild pressure and with the fingers on either side of the spine, place one hand over the top of the fingers. Then, in a gentle sawing-like action, rock the fingers back and forth while moving gently down the spine to the sacrum. Repeat this procedure two more times.

The next technique will take a little practice. Beginning at the sacrum, with your thumbs on either side of the spine, you will use the Vita Flex technique working up the spine approximately a thumb's width apart with each move up to the atlas. With the thumbs on each side of the spine, nail side up and slightly angled out, rock the thumbs up to where the thumbs are straight up with the joints slightly bent. Then, apply a mild pressure straight down. Continue to roll your thumbs slightly over onto the nails, and then release. Move your thumbs up about a thumb's width, and apply the same technique. Do this all the way to the atlas, and then repeat two more times.

Step 4

Apply five or six drops of **marjoram** and **Aroma Siez** to each side of the spine, away from the spine, into the muscle tissue all over the back. Work these oils in, using a gentle massage to smooth and relax, working all over the back for a few minutes. After the oils have been massaged in well, rest approximately five minutes. Then apply **Ortho Ease** over the entire area of the back and legs.

Step 5

Take a hand towel that is folded into thirds lengthwise, and soak it in hot water. Wring it out, then lay it along the entire length of the spine. Take a dry towel and fold it in half lengthwise and place it over the wet towel. **Pay close attention because the back can become very hot!** The heat will generally build slowly in intensity to where it will peak in 5 to 8 minutes. It will then cool right down to where it feels pleasant. The water in the towel drives the oils deeper into the skin. The more out of balance, the more virus or bacteria activity in the body; or, the more inflammation in the spine, the hotter the area will become along the spine. Some people will experience no heat, while for others it will be mild and very pleasant. Still, for others it may be hot and a little uncomfortable. **Pay attention to what the recipient is saying.** Ask questions.

If it becomes too uncomfortable, remove the towels and apply V-6 Mixing Oil on the back. Then work it in. This will usually remove the heat within minutes.

After putting on the towels, wait a few minutes to see how the person is responding. If the back does not become very hot, ask the person to roll over so the back is against the towel on the table. This usually creates more heat.

Step 6

Take the four oils of **birch, cypress, basil** and **peppermint,** in that order, and apply 2 to 3 drops of each oil along the inside of the lower legs along the shin bone from the bottom of the knee area to the top of the big toes. Apply one at a time, and layer each oil in before applying the next oil.

Place the fingers of one hand along the inside of the shin bone just below the knee. Work the fingers down to the ankle, and then along the foot up to the top of the big toe using the Vita Flex technique. Roll your fingers up and then over onto the nails of the fingers, applying slightly more pressure at the top of the roll and releasing as you come over onto the nails. Short nails would be appreciated by the person on whom you are working. Repeat this procedure three times on each leg.

Step 7

This next step works best with two people. Have the individual assisting stand at the feet of the person on whom you are working and hold each leg tightly just above the ankles. You stand at the head and gently put your right hand under the base of the head. Place your left hand around the chin, then gently pull to create a slight tension. Hold this traction for several minutes, but do not pull hard. The person at the feet will be the anchor, holding the same position while the person at the head begins a mild rocking of pulling and releasing, pulling and releasing, etc. This may take anywhere from 4 to 8 minutes. This procedure can be tiring, so you must exercise patience. As you get a feel for the whole application, you will sense what is needed.

Step 8

Have the person on the table roll back so he or she is again face down. Rest the head in the head-cradle of the massage table again and make sure the person is lying straight. Remove the towels and then examine the spine. Corrections may or may not be visible. At this point you may add another therapy, as desired. Sometimes the desired results are not immediate, yet the body will continue to respond for days, at which time you may begin to see gradual changes.

This is the basic Raindrop Therapy, although there are several variations on which I have been working. However, these are not easy to explain, and require class instruction and demonstration. Everybody is different, and what works for one may not work for another. Different body types respond to the applications in ways you may not expect. Learn to be sensitive to the person on whom you are working so that you can respond to his or her needs.

The question is often asked, "How long does the application last?" Again, everybody responds differently. Generally speaking, the level of health and proper diet are key factors, as are exercise and mental attitude. One application may last months for one person, but then for another it may be necessary to have the application repeated every week until the body begins to respond. The key is to retrain the body. In some cases, you will have to develop a new memory in the tissue in order for the body to stay were it should be. This may take a few weeks, or even a full year.

Spinal alignment may have a completely different look when the individual is lying down, rather than sitting. There is more torque on the spine in a sitting or standing position, so these are the positions in which X-rays are usually taken. There may appear to be a total correction when the individual is lying down, and then appear to be crooked when they are in the sitting position. This variance is normal, and may be apparent until a total retraining of the tissue can occur. The object is to achieve straightening in all positions. The Raindrop Therapy is a powerful tool that can not only assist therapists, but help everyone achieve a balance in the body.

The Essential 7 Kit

As people become acquainted with essential oils, they always say that there are so many oils, and so many uses, that they don't know where to begin. To make it easier for someone to understand essential oils, I put together what I call the **Essential 7.** All seven oils can be diffused, worn as perfume, applied to the Vita Flex points on the feet, added to bath water, applied on location, or used with body and foot massage. These are as follows:

1. **Lavender** has universal purpose, and is the application most recognized for burns, headaches, cuts, bruises, skin irritation, insomnia, itching, PMS, stress and hair loss. The fragrance is calming, relaxing and balancing, both physically and emotionally.

2. **Lemon** has been found to promote leukocyte formation, to dissolve cellulite, to increase lymphatic function, and to promote a sense of well-being. It is beneficial for the skin, serves in the purification of air and water, and dissolves gum and grease spots.

3. **Peppermint** has been found to improve mental accuracy, and soothe the respiratory system. It may also relieve nausea, fever, vomiting and acid stomach. In addition, it is used for air and water purification.

4. **Purification** is an oil blend that helps purify the air neutralizing mildew, cigarette smoke, and other obnoxious odors found in homes, offices, and other confined areas.

5. **Joy** is an exotic blend of **ylang ylang, bergamot, citrus** and pure **rose oil.** These oils produce a magnetic energy that enhances self-love, and brings joy to the heart.

6. **Peace & Calming** is used to promote relaxation and a sense of peace after a stressful day. When diffused in the home, it may help calm overactive and hard-to-manage children.

7. **Pane Away** may help to reduce inflammation, promoting healthy circulation and healing, thus reducing pain. Many people have had great relief from arthritis symptoms, sports injuries, sprains, muscle spasms, and bumps and bruises.

Golden Touch Kits For Physical Application

With all we have discussed thus far, it is obvious that the oils have many different applications. In order to help people understand how they work together, I have tried to put the oils together according to their physical, emotional and spiritual application. **Golden Touch 1** and **Golden Touch 2** work on the physical level.

Golden Touch 1 Kit

The electrical frequencies of the essential oils and their antimicrobial, antioxidant, and immune-stimulating properties, have been the missing link to re-establishing optimum health. The formulas have been specifically formulated to create a frequency that will work in a harmonic application with the constituents in the oils. When correctly applied, they may help improve respiratory, digestive and endocrine function, as well as prevent fungus, bacteria and microbial mutation.

1. **Endo Flex** may support the entire endocrine system, assisting with hormonal balance, thyroid support and balancing metabolism. The blend has been reported to encourage weight loss. Apply on Vita Flex points of the feet.

2. **Di-Tone** has been reported to assist in relieving digestive irregularity and disturbances, such as an upset stomach, belching and bloating. Apply on Vita Flex points of the feet, make a compress for the stomach, or put a couple of drops behind the ears for morning sickness.

3. **Melrose** has antiseptic-like properties when used topically for cleansing cuts, scrapes, burns, rashes and bruised tissue. It may also help prevent growth of bacteria, fungus or infection. Apply on location and diffuse to dispel odors.

4. **Thieves** is an oil blend that was formulated from the research about the thieves during the 16th century plague in England who rubbed oils all over their bodies to protect themselves while they were robbing the dead and dying. The assumption was that these oils strengthened the immune system, thus protecting them from the disease. **Thieves** may be massaged on the feet and diffused in the home and work environment. However, diffuse only one-half hour at a time.

5. **Juva Flex** is formulated with oils that have been known to support liver and lymphatic system detoxification, as well as to support digestion. Apply on the Vita Flex points of the feet. **Juva Flex** and **Di-Tone** work extremely well together.

6. **Raven** helps fight respiratory disease and infections. It works well alternating with **R.C.,** and as a companion to **ImmuPower.** It may be applied on chest, neck, back, feet and diffused.

7. **R.C.** is blended with oils traditionally used throughout Europe for relief of respiratory congestion and sinusitis. **R.C.** may be massaged on the chest, neck and feet. Diffusing may help decongest and relieve allergy-type symptoms such as coughs, sore throats and lung congestion.

Golden Touch 2 Kit

The electrical frequencies and oxygenating molecular activity of these essential oil formulas may help contribute to pain relief, improved memory, and experience more complete organ and hormone function. These formulas have been specially created to obtain harmonic frequency with the constituents in the oils. When this is accomplished, they are able to help improve cardiovascular and hormonal functions; reduce mental fatigue, headaches, and pain. They likewise improve memory, promote skin elasticity during birthing, and promote general skin improvement.

1. **Aroma Life** is formulated with oils that have been traditionally used to support heart function and regulate the circulatory system. In combination with **helichrysum** and **cypress,** it may help reduce the symptoms of varicose veins. Apply all over body, and massage on the Vita Flex points on the feet.

2. **Relieve It** has oils with high anti-inflammatory action that were formulated together for the benefit of relieving deep tissue pain. Apply on location.

3. **Mister** is used to decongest the prostate and promote greater hormonal balance. Some women have found it to reduce hot flashes. Apply to Vita Flex points on ankles and diffuse.

4. **My-Grain** is formulated with oils traditionally used to relieve headaches, nausea, depression and problems related to severe migraine headaches. Rub a few drops in the palms of your hands, and then cup your hand over your nose and inhale. Massage on temples, back of neck and on forehead. Keep away from eyes.

5. **Gentle Baby** is a beautiful combination for mothers and babies. It is comforting, soothing, relaxing and may be beneficial during the birthing process, as well as in helping to relieve stress during pregnancy. The oils have been traditionally used in European cosmetics to enhance the youthful appearance of the skin. It may be diffused or used in massage.

6. **Clarity** has been reported to be beneficial for memory retention and mental alertness, as well as a stimulant for someone experiencing low energy. It may be diffused, worn as a perfume, or used in bathing. It is an excellent combination with **En-R-Gee** for night driving.

7. **Dragon Time** helps women alleviate those uncomfortable days of the month, reducing cramps, and still allowing them to feel feminine. It may be rubbed over the lower back region, used as a compress on location, and applied on Vita Flex points on the ankle.

Emotions and the Essential Oil Connection

*"The cure of the part should not be attempted without
treatment of the whole,
and also no attempt should be made to cure the
body without the soul, and therefore
if the head and body are to be well you must begin by curing the mind:
that is the first thing....For this is the great error of our day
in the treatment of the human body, that physicians
separate the soul from the body."*

Plato, Chronicles 156 e

Frankincense is mentioned 52 times in the *Bible,* of which 32 times it is referred to as incense. The Greek/Hebrew translation of incense means frankincense. **Frankincense** has been recognized since ancient times as the *holy anointing oil.* It obtained this legendary title because the ancient priests and physicians found they could rub it on sick people and they would almost immediately get well. They also found that when they were inhaling it, the fragrance from the atmosphere through evaporation, or through the burning of the incense, increased their spiritual awareness and made them feel more spiritually "in tune."

Modern science now shows us that **frankincense has the ability to increase the oxygen around the pineal and pituitary gland,** therefore stimulating the pineal gland through which we communicate spiritually. **Frankincense** has been found to help alleviate manic depressive symptoms. Because it is high in sesquiterpene activity, it has the ability to work as an immune stimulant. It also contains anti-carcinogenic properties, and is now being studied for its effectiveness in the possible treatment of cancer.

I discovered the emotional benefits of essential oils quite by accident. This was an area that was rarely mentioned in my travels around the world. Most everyone I asked, hoping to learn more about the emotional connection to oils, would scoff at the idea. However, when I was testing different oils, such as **lavender** and **Roman chamomile,** in the clinic for anti-allergy effects, I noticed that the patients became rather complacent, relaxed and calm. These were the same patients who, an hour earlier, were either depressed or hyperactive.

One of my patients was suffering from suicidal depression, hormonal imbalance and severe allergies. Nothing seemed to be working for her. Her severe depression was like a block to everything. One afternoon she asked if there was anything that might help her as she was, "ready to check out of life!" I had just created a new oil formula, now called **Inspiration,** which was designed to help the mind move into a quiet space for spiritual communication. She stretched out on the massage table, and I rubbed it on her feet and just held them, not really knowing what to do next. I was just hoping she could relax. Within one minute she started breathing heavily and began crying with acceleration. She then started to release an old memory of the time she had had an abortion, and was clutching her throat while gasping for air. I then put two drops each of **geranium, ylang ylang, lavender** and **sandalwood** on the crown of her head, which I later formulated and called **Release.** She coughed and gasped for air, then gradually started breathing normally. I then instructed her to rub the oils of **rose, ylang ylang, mandarin, spruce,** etc., over the heart area; and after a few drops, which I later formulated and called **Joy,** she quit crying and settled down. She then said, "I am free. I can now go forward." She then told me that when she had the abortion, the umbilical cord was wrapped around the neck of the fetus. Additionally, she had gone through three failed marriages, and had three businesses collapse and countless job failures. That was nine years ago. Today, she has a very happy marriage, and owns a successful business.

Many of us today are not aware of how old trauma memory can alter our lives and create disease. After the experience referred to above, I conducted blood studies before and after using essential oils for the releasing of negative programming. I could detect significant changes in the blood cells within 20 minutes. From that experience, I went further into the research of the use of essential oils and their emotional benefits.

The three photos that follow are the results of a very early experiment I conducted. Photo A is a picture of the blood from one of the nurses who worked in the clinic in Mexico, who had a bad case of allergies and candida. It shows one dying nutrifile, which indicates that the immune system was very weak. High levels of bacteria from the candida were also quite evident. Photo B shows a healthier blood specimen showing two strong nutrifiles and very well-defined red blood cells. As my nurse held photo B, she closed her eyes, and took a deep breath of lavender oil. She then opened her eyes and refocused, then again closed them and inhaled – all the while visualizing the cells of

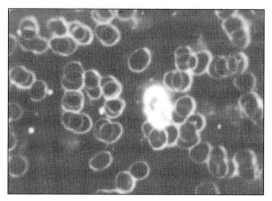

Photo A – One dying nutrifile.

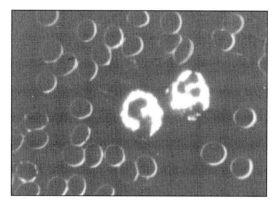

Photo B – Two strong nutrifiles and well-defined red blood cells.

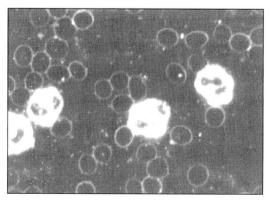

Photo C – Duplication of nutrifiles from photo B.

photo B to be those of her own. After 20 minutes, another blood sample was taken, and the results were amazing. As you can see in photo C, there is an exact duplication. This was another new beginning in the exploration of essential oils.

While conducting research in Egypt, I learned that the ancient Egyptians practiced a ritual called **"Cleansing the Flesh and Blood of Evil Deities."** In our language, we would refer to it as the releasing of negative emotions and memory trauma. Today, we would also call this procedure psychological therapy or emotional clearing. This ancient ritual took three days to complete with two facilitators using certain essential oils and oil baths. Over the years, since this discovery, I have seen hundreds of lives changed and people freed from emotional devastation as they went through this process. Using oil formulations I have made, I have subsequently developed a program for various emotional applications. It is rewarding to me to be able to bring this ancient custom back so that those who desire may experience the incredible benefit of emotional freedom it brings. Our greatest challenge is recognizing our own emotional bondage. By being able to break our old emotional bonds and negative thought processes – which is what I believe is meant in the *Bible* by the phrase "breaking the lineage of iniquity" – we will be able to go forward in our lives and achieve our full potential.

The emotions of the mind are the most elusive part of the human body. Research has only begun to delve into the realm of the subconscious mind and how emotions affect every aspect of our lives. The ancient Egyptians believed that if they didn't clear the body and mind of negative influences before dying, they could not progress into the next life. Nor could they return to this world to enter back into the body they had

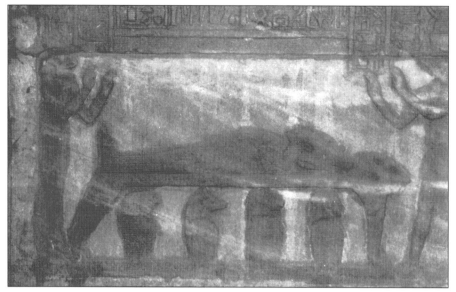

Mummification ceremony.

Egyptian ritual clearing – "Cleansing the Flesh and Blood of Evil Deities."

left in the tomb. In order to progress into the spirit realm, they had to seek favor of their gods by going through this cleansing ritual with the oils.

The two photos shown depict two very specific rituals. Photo A depicts the mummification ceremony. The four alabaster containers shown under the bed contain the internal organs that were removed for this process. The oils of **cedarwood** and **myrrh,** mixed with herbs, were put into the urns.

In photo B, you can see a completely different ritual. I first learned about this ritual in the Great Pyramid, in 1993; but of which I found no evidence until a year later. In March of 1994, while walking with a tour group of 62 people in the Temple of Isis, on the Island of Philae, one of the guards told me that he would show me that for which I was searching. He indicated that there was a special room that was forbidden for people to see, simply because very sacred rituals had been practiced there by his ancestors. He then stated that I was to learn about these rituals in order to help many people. I felt this guard was really just a "used car salesman" and refused to go with him, thinking all he wanted was "bacschese" (money). Twice he came to me, and twice I walked away from him. He was persistent, however, and came looking for me a third time, insisting that I had come for special information that he could show me. I felt a little queasy in the stomach as he very soberly and intently insisted he knew why I was there, and if I would go with him, he would show me this special room.

He was intent on finding me in the crowd, even though I was trying to elude him. After the third time, I was reminded of an experience in 1973 when I had been warned three times to leave the mountain I was on, when I was badly injured by a falling tree. I quickly looked around to see if there were any trees close by, and decided maybe I had better listen. I then returned with the guard to the temple to a darkened corridor, where he unlocked a steel gate leading to an almost-hidden stairway. He motioned for me to quickly go inside, and I instantly felt a sense of panic when I looked back and saw that he was on the other side of the gate looking through at me. Once he was certain that no one saw us enter, he quickly stepped through the gate and locked it behind us. He motioned for me to ascend the stairs; and as I reached the top, he pushed past me and went over to a small door. He then nodded for me to come and see. As I stepped through the doorway, my eyes beheld the pictographs on the walls of the very thing I was told about the year before. I felt my knees weaken, and the whole world seemed to start spinning as I collapsed on the floor with a totally overwhelming feeling. Then I heard his voice as though he were a million miles away saying, "This you come to Egypt to find, no? You special, it ok you take picture, you take movie picture, for you ok."

The temple of Isis on the island of Philae where I was taken into the sacred room.

I was later told that this room was very sacred and forbidden for anyone to see; and yet, there it was before me, the entire ritual of the three-day cleansing. You can see the person on the bed has one arm up over his head, while the person assisting is touching the feet. The hieroglyphic is clear enough to see the torment the individual is experiencing as he goes through the emotional cleansing.

Today, people are extremely handicapped emotionally, and are continually looking for ways of clearing these negative emotions. They are unable to progress in life and achieve their goals and dreams due to the trauma of emotional and physical abuse.

These formulas were created based on the research of ancient Egyptian ritual clearing. This research is on-going, and new knowledge is continually coming forth. Already hundreds of people are experiencing freedom from their emotional bondage and are going forward in life with new found excitement, happiness and the joy of greater accomplishment.

Feelings Kit

1. **Valor** should be the first formula used and applied to the bottom of the feet when starting an emotional clearing. It helps balance the energies within the body, helping to give courage, confidence and self-esteem.

2. **3 Wise Men** was formulated to open the subconscious mind through pineal stimulation to release deep-seated trauma encoded in the DNA of the cells. The oils bring a sense of grounding and uplifting through emotional releasing, and elevate spiritual consciousness. Place a couple of drops on the crown of the head. It may be diffused, or worn as a perfume.

3. **Harmony** is an exquisite blend of 12 oils. These oils promote physical and emotional healing, bringing about a harmonic balance to the energy centers of the body. Once this is accomplished, energy flows more efficiently throughout the body. It helps reduce stress and creates an overall feeling of well-being. Place a couple of drops on the energy meridians either directly on or along the sides of the body. It may be diffused, or worn as a perfume.

4. **Forgiveness** has high electrical frequencies, which may help release negative memory and emotions in order to forgive and forget. Apply around navel, or wear as a perfume.

5. **Joy** is an exotic blend of ylang ylang, bergamot and pure rose oil. It produces a magnetic energy to attract love and enhance the frequency of self-love, bringing joy to the heart. Apply over the heart, diffuse, or wear as a perfume.

6. **Present Time** has an empowering fragrance that gives a feeling of being "in the moment." One can only go forward and progress when in the present time. Apply over the thymus, diffuse, or wear as a perfume or aftershave.

7. **Release** may stimulate a sense of harmony and balance within the mind and body, and may help to release anger and frustration. When this is accomplished it brings about a sense of peace and emotional well-being. Apply over the liver area.

8. **Inner Child** is a formula that will have an effect in several different ways. When children have been abused and misused, they become disconnected from their inner child or identity. This, in turn, causes confusion, and can contribute to multiple personalities. Sometimes

these problems don't manifest themselves until early- to mid-adult years, often labeled as mid-life crisis, business and personal failures. The fragrance of this formula may stimulate the amygdala, bringing about memory response. This may help one to reconnect with the inner-self or one's identity, which is one of the first steps to finding emotional balance. Apply around navel and nose.

9. **Grounding** may be helpful when we have disconnected from reality, either because we are excited about new ideas, or because we want to escape into a protective fantasy. When disconnected or not grounded, it is easy to make choices which lead to unfortunate circumstances, such as bad relationships and bad business decisions. We escape because we don't have anchoring or awareness to know how to deal with the emotions. This formula helps stabilize and ground us in order to deal logically, with reality in a peaceful manner. It may be applied to the brain stem, back of neck and sternum.

10. **Hope** is what everyone needs in order to go forward in life. Hopelessness can cause a loss of vision, goals and dreams. This blend helps to reconnect with a feeling of strength and grounding, restoring hope for tomorrow and helping us go forward. It may also help overcome suicidal depression. Massage on outer edge of the ears.

11. **SARA** has a fragrance that, when inhaled, may enable one to relax into a mental state whereby one may be able to release and let go of the memory trauma of sexual and/or ritual abuse. Apply over energy centers, Vita Flex points, temples and nose.

12. **White Angelica** is a combination of 18 oils, some of which were used during ancient times to increase the aura around the body. It brings

a delicate sense of strength and protection, creating a feeling of wholeness in the realm of one's own spirituality and oneness with the Creator. Its frequency protects against the bombardment of negative energy. May be worn as a perfume, especially on the shoulders, or diffused.

7th Heaven Kit

In our world today, we sometimes experience periods of great confusion, uncertainty, and insecurity in our lives regarding our spiritual direction. There are television programs, books and people quite willing to tell us how we should think and act. However, there is so much information and direction that it often becomes difficult to sort through the bombardment, leaving us vulnerable to many falsehoods. One's spirituality is the most guarded and intimate feeling we have about ourselves. We have to sort things out and find peace and balance with our own understanding.

These beautiful formulas have been used with great joy and meaningful experience. They contain oils that have been used and recognized for thousands of years to bring balance to the pineal and pituitary glands. In time, they help us attain a higher spiritual frequency. These formulas work extremely well in companionship with the emotional formulas in the Feelings kit.

1. **Awaken** helps balance one's state of mind and emotions through self-adjustment, by allowing a gentle change toward renewal and balance. The oils contained in this formula awaken one to inner knowing in order to change and make a transition in life, enabling a person to reach his or her highest potential. It may be diffused and worn as a perfume or aftershave.

2. **Dream Catcher** may enhance dreams and visualization, promoting greater potential to achieve your dreams and stay on your path, thus protecting you from negative dreams that might steal your vision. It may be worn or diffused. Sprinkle a couple of drops on your pillow at night for a delightful night's rest.

3. **Gathering** was created out of the need to help us overcome the bombardment of chaotic frequencies that alter our focus and take us off our path of higher achievements. **Galbanum,** a favorite oil of Moses, has a strong effect with **frankincense** and **sandalwood** in gathering our emotional and spiritual thoughts. It helps us focus and hold to the "iron rod," which enables us to achieve our highest potential. It may be worn on the temples and neck, and is wonderful to diffuse.

4. **Humility** is an integral ingredient in having forgiveness and seeking a closer relationship with God. Having humility and forgiveness help us to heal ourselves and our earth. (Chronicles 7:14) This beautiful formula, through frequency and fragrance, may help you to find that special place where your own healing may begin. It is a powerful companion to **Forgiveness** and **Gathering.** It may be worn or diffused.

5. **Inspiration** is a combination of oils that have been used traditionally by the Eastern and North American native people for increasing spirituality. These oils have been found effective for enhancing prayer and inner awareness. It is wonderful to wear, as well as to diffuse.

6. **Sacred Mountain** represents the sacred feeling of the mountains. The oils are extracted from conifers, such as **fir, spruce** and **pine,** and have been reported to bring about a feeling of protection, strength and security. They also represent the ancient Eastern philosophies that emphasize finding that sacredness within oneself. May be worn and diffused.

7. **White Angelica** is a combination of 18 oils, some of which were used during ancient times to increase the aura around the body. It brings a delicate sense of strength and protection, creating a feeling of wholeness in the realm of one's own spirituality and oneness with the Creator. Its frequency protects against the bombardment of negative energy. Put on shoulders and wear as perfume, or diffuse.

Essential Oils as Food Flavoring and Vitamin Supplementation

I wouldn't be surprised to find that at least 80 percent of the American population is constipated. Most people seem to have digestive problems, such as gas, bloating, indigestion, morning sickness, etc. Then they take a little bottle of the essential oil formula **Di-Tone,** which contains peppermint oil, rub it on their stomach, and are surprised that their symptoms go away almost immediately. It is wonderful to know that we don't have to ingest the oils in order for them to work. However, when used as a food additive, they increase the absorption of the food. I discovered in clinical practice, while doing bacteriology studies with the blood, that there was an incredible amount of food bacteria in the blood serum. I knew this because: (1) it didn't digest, and (2) it couldn't get through the cell wall because of low oxygen levels. When we put the oils in the food products, we didn't find any undigested food bacteria in the blood. Through these studies, I discovered several things were happening:

1. The food digested better. Essential oils, like **rosemary, aniseed, juniper, peppermint,** and **tarragon,** aided in digestive enzyme secretion.

2. Essential oils digested and prevented unfriendly bacteria growth.

3. Essential oils acted as a catalyst, and were soluble with the lipids in the membranes. Therefore, they went directly inside the cell and piggybacked nutrients of similar harmonic frequency and value in the cell at the same time.

4. The oxygenating molecules increased cell metabolism and helped in balancing the pH of the cell for increased nutritional intake of the food in the body.

5. Because various oils contain phenylpropanes, the precursor of amino acids, they helped strengthen all body functions.

My next challenge, which took two and one-half years to discover, was to find a method of adding the oils to my herbal food supplements. One of the reasons I began to formulate supplements, myself, was because in my clinic I would see patients passing herbs and vitamin tablets and capsules whole during their colonics (colon irrigating), after having ingested them 6 to 12 days prior to their colonics.

When distilled, essential oils contain all the healing nutrients, oxygenating molecules, amino acid precursors, coenzyme A factors, trace amounts of minerals, enzymes, vitamins, hormones, etc., in a concentrated form. However, today, man cuts the herbs and dehydrates them, destroying 90 percent of the healing nutrients and the oxygen, which delivers the nutrients to the cells. Then we wonder why herbs don't have the same potency they used to have. If you take the blood out of the human body, you have a corpse. If you take the oil out of the plant, you have only the fiber devoid of its healing life force. When I began to understand this, it seemed to me that we needed that life force back in the plant. I then began to experiment with oils as a food additive and flavoring agent. This was the most revolutionary development in the health food industry.

VitaGreen, the first food product with essential oils, was formulated to bring the blood back to an alkalinity pH; simply because disease cannot develop in an alkaline free-flowing blood stream. Barley grass juice is the highest alkaline food we have. Alfalfa sprouts are 52 percent alkaline protein. Spirulina, Norwegian kelp, bee pollen, amino acids and essential oils were formulated during my clinical practice to help those who could not digest food, to balance blood sugar, and to help those who had a greater need for more pre-digested alkaline protein. Before I put the oils in **VitaGreen,** my patients only had 42 percent blood absorption in 24 hrs. After I put the oils in this supplement, the blood absorption increased to 64 percent in 30 minutes, then 86 percent in one hour. This began to make amazing changes with my patients, and we saw the immune function "kick in" from **VitaGreen** alone. I concluded this was happening because the cells were now receiving nutrition that they had previously not been able to assimilate.

When you properly feed the body, it can heal itself. However, I have seen people supposedly eating well, yet dying from disease – because they could not get the nutrition into the cell because the food was devoid of its natural nutritional delivery agent. The oils are nature's most natural catalyst and delivery agent.

The next formulas into which I put the oils were **ComforTone and I.C.P.** I formulated these to assist in cleansing the intestinal tract of toxic debris and parasites, which are hosts for many diseases. Parasites are very difficult to get rid of which I didn't realize until I assisted in the operating room with some of my patients who required surgery. It was there that I witnessed the grotesque sight of a human body eaten alive by worms. The first time I saw this tragedy was with a patient who several years earlier had been diagnosed with parasites by Bernard

Jensen, D.C. This patient had been eating herbs, garlic and pumpkin seeds for seven years in an effort to rid herself of them. However, we literally removed over four quarts of worms from her abdomen, many the size of my little finger. This experience motivated me to make these two formulas, each containing seven oils. **Patchouly,** for example, aids in the digestion of toxic waste. **Tarragon, ginger** and **mugwort** help the garlic oil absorb into the intestinal lining, penetrating the parasite pockets or nests. **Rosemary** kills fungus and aids in digestive secretion. **Peppermint** is antiparasitic, and soothes an inflamed colon and reduces fever. After adding the oils, patients started passing parasites within 12-13 hours. We have also had reports that **ComforTone and I.C.P.** bring about the same results in animals.

Body Balance was a formula I made to feed my patients who could not eat solid foods. It was difficult to nutritionally support the body on liquids alone, so the development of **Body Balance** required great study and selection of the right nutrients. Many people avoided the soy isolate because they claimed it was not digestible and, therefore, many health food manufacturers threw it out. However, the pure soy isolate is 92 percent pure protein. We found that by fractionating the isolate, it was easier to digest. I then added more enzymes using grade A fructose as a sweetener with **grapefruit** oil, giving **Body Balance** a great flavor. Five other citrus oils were added, which have been found to help decongest the lymphatic system and increase leukocyte production. Pure fructose is the only sweetener that is really safe for diabetics, and doesn't ferment in the stomach. It also converts to pure protein glucose sugar.

It was easy to monitor the progress of our patients and the effectiveness of the formulas when they spent two to six weeks "in house" in a clinical environment. If a formula didn't appear to be working, I could change it until it *did* work. My clinical practice gave me the great foundation for the development of the important work I am now doing.

At that time, however, I began to formulate programs so people could get benefits at home. The first program developed for individual use at home is now called **The Cleansing Trio.** This program contains **ComforTone, I.C. P. and Megazyme. Megazyme** is an enzyme complex designed to aid in the digestion of toxic material, as well as to help with the cleansing and promotion of better assimilation. The first step to good health is cleansing the body and then feeding it good nutrients.

The second program is called **The Body Balancing Trio,** which contains **VitaGreen, Body Balance and Master Formula His and Hers. Body Balance** is great in water alone, but one can also add different oils for flavoring, such as **orange, grapefruit, peppermint, nutmeg,** etc., with each bringing its different benefits. **Master Formula His or Hers** is a multi-vitamin formulation made through a 16-stage synergistic suspension isolation to assure that the antagonistic nutrients like the B vitamins don't interfere with the synergistic ones, yet can be put into one tablet.

A third program is for building the immune system. I spent many years developing the **ImmuneTune** formula. Beta Carotene has always been respected for its ability to help the body build antibodies, white blood cells, and prevent premature aging and cancer. I also examined all the difficulties we have when fighting degenerative disease, and wanted to incorporate all the ingredients that would help in this area. As a result, I added pantothenic acid, biotin, and coenzyme Q10. These nutrients are always lacking in people who have degenerative disease. Proanthocyanidins found in grape pit and pine bark combined with essential oils in an herbal base complete the formula.

Proanthocyanidins is very interesting and needs clarification because of the great controversy regarding its effectiveness. Most of that which is sold in America is of a very low quality. Again, Americans are more concerned about the cost rather than the quality. In reality, however, the cheaper product costs more in the end. Pure pine bark extract, which costs $6,800 per kilo, has to come from the inner bark, or the phloem, of the tree. This inner bark is where the active O.P.C. (proanthocyanidins) is found, which is the flavonoid responsible for most of the activity. The other three grades of bark have only 6 percent active O.P.C., or less, depending on how it is processed. It sells for $1,200 per kilo, so the price certainly reflects the quality. I found from Dr. Masquelier's work that the redwine grape pit is even higher in O.P.C. activity, and therefore, by combining the two, the potential results are even greater. The essential oils increase the bio-availability of the nutrients and assist in their delivery to the cells. When combining **ImmuneTune** with **Radex** (which is a powerful free radical scavenger containing super oxide dismutase), with essential oils and **Super C,** we have an incredible formula for the immune system.

Another ever-increasing problem today is that of sexual inadequacies and dysfunction. The increased chemicals in our environment, air, food, water, as well as our stressful lifestyles, all contribute to glandular and hormonal imbalance. Depression and fatigue are two of the primary symptoms, and many people suffer even to the point of destroying their relationships.

In an effort to help those who suffer in these areas, I created the **Sensation Trio,** which has the **Sensation Hand & Body Lotion, Sensation Bath Gel and the Sensation Massage Oil.** The oils contained in this trio have been tested and found to contain natural coenzyme

A factors that are responsible for natural hormone production. The pineal and pituitary glands, which are largely responsible for the production of hormones, are stimulated by the fragrance through the olfactory nerve. By combining the stimulation of fragrance and touch, the sensation of feelings during those intimate times is greatly enhanced.

In today's world, our skin is constantly affected by pollution and harmful chemicals that can cause allergic reactions and skin irritations. With the ever-changing conditions of our ozone and environmental pollution, scientists have discovered that the UV Rays of the sun have been substantially altered. In turn, this makes sun exposure one of the leading causes of abnormal skin pigmentation, sunspots, moles and discoloration. The ever-present chemicals in our environment also affect the photosynthesis of the skin, causing reactions such as itching, rashes, scaly and flaky skin, etc.

One of the Egyptian secrets was to combine vegetable, nut and essential oils for daily skin and hair care. This kept their skin soft and silky, and their hair moist, preventing brittleness and breaking. The Egyptians were recognized throughout the world as having the most beautiful skin and hair. Subsequently, these skin care ingredients were adopted by other cultures, such as the Greeks and Romans.

The **Sensation Trio** not only gives the skin a silky, youthful feeling, but its beautiful fragrance may stimulate feelings of romance and desire.

Every time I make a new formula, new ideas come to me, and I find myself actively engaged in my laboratory to the exclusion of everything else beyond the closed door. I have found great excitement and immense satisfaction in being able to put different ingredients together, creating formulas and watching to see how they work. I am always anxious for the feedback from those using my new products. I have not only been interested in the nurturing of the body from the inside, but also caring for the body from the outside.

I felt it was important to make shampoos and conditioners free of sodium lauryl sulphate, which is one of the leading causes of diminished eyesight in children, as well as allergies in adults. By putting the essential oils in shampoo, I have found that they help oxygenate and cleanse as well as feed the hair shaft and hair follicle. Our shampoos contain the various oils of **lavender, ylang ylang, cedarwood,** and **rosemary.** These oils have been reported to help in the prevention of hair loss and the improvement of hair growth. **Sandalwood** decreases graying, and rosemary lightens and increases the blond look. Because of their chelating action, some oils may tend to relax a perm a little.

I developed allergy symptoms to hand soap from all the chemicals I had in my body from the prescription drugs I took for more than seven years after my accident. For this reason, I had a vested interest in making chemical-free soaps. It is an absolute treat to start each day with **Morning Start Bath and Shower Gel,** or before going to bed to enjoy a peaceful bath with **Evening Peace, Relaxation or Sensation Bath and Shower Gel.** It is wonderful to nurture the body with life-giving substances, so I have continued to develop more and more products to help protect us and give us a fighting chance against the eroding environment.

When we recognize the incredible attributes of **essential oils** with their **high antioxidant properties, their high antiviral, antibacterial and anti-infectious properties, their high antimicrobial activity, and their high immune-stimulating power,** we must conclude that essential oils are truly one of God's greatest gifts to mankind.

Reference Guide

Essential Oil Constituents

The following is a list of the various families of chemical constituents. Individual chemical families have several different constituents.

Aldehydes are various organic compounds, which are highly reactive, typified by acetaldehydes and characterized by the group C-H-O (Carbon, Hydrogen, Oxygen). They are anti-infectious and sedative. When inhaled, they are calming. When applied topically, however, they are usually irritating. Citral is an example.

Azulene prevents discharge of histamine (amino acid) from the tissues by activating the pituitary-adrenal system, causing the release of cortisone. It may be useful for asthmatic conditions. Azulene causes histamine release-activating cellular resistance and speeds up the process of healing. It contains trace elements of blue mineral and copper. Azulene also stimulates liver regeneration, and is anti-inflammatory.

Bisabolol is the strongest of the sesquiterpene alcohols. It is anti-inflammatory, antibacterial, anti-mycotic and ulcer-protective (preventative). It works well as a fixative as found in **chamomile** oil.

Carvacrol is antiseptic, energizing, and possibly anti-cancerous.

Citral is part of the aldehyde family. It is sedative and anti-infectious, and has an antiviral application, as with melissa oil when applied topically on herpes simplex.

Esters are the compound resulting from the reaction of an alcohol with an acid. The reaction is called esterification and is accompanied by the yield of H_2O along with the esters. Since esters are not very soluble in water, water may be added to the distillation, thus removing the water and the alcohol. Upon redistillation, all of the water will be distilled, thus producing pure esters.

Eugenol comes from the phenol group and is very antiseptic and stimulating. Because the properties are so strong, they are sometimes toxic to the central nervous system. Cinnamon leaf is distilled to extract the eugenol.

Flavonoids show beneficial effects on the capillaries. In chamomile, by inhibiting methyl transferase, epinephrine effects are prolonged, and the pituitary-adrenal axis is stimulated.

Farnesol is anti-inflammatory, antibacterial, and dermatophile (Latin: having an affinity for skin). It is also good for mucous membranes, and prevents bacterial growth from perspiration.

Farnesene is part of the terpene family, and is antiviral in action.

Ketones are sometimes mucolytic and neuro-toxic when isolated from other constituents, and should be used with caution. They stimulate cell regeneration, promote the formation of tissue, and liquefy mucous. They are helpful with such conditions as dry asthma, cold, flu and dry cough.

Limonene has strong antiviral properties.

Linalool (Linalol) is antibacterial, relieves discomfort, tones without irritating, stimulates the immune system, is sedating, and works as a diuretic.

Monoterpenes include pinene, camphene, sabinene and limonene.

Phenols are antiseptic and kill bacteria. Cresol, thymol or carvacol found in thyme oil, are very hot to the skin. They contain high levels of oxygenating molecules, and have antioxidant properties.

Sesquiterpenes are antiseptic and anti-inflammatory. They work as a liver and gland stimulant, and contain caryophylene and valencene. Recent research from the universities of Berlin and Vienna show increased oxygenation around the pineal and pituitary glands.

Terpenes inhibit accumulation of toxins as well as discharge the toxins in certain organs, especially the liver and kidneys.

Terpene Alcohols are antibacterial, stimulate the immune system, and work as diuretics and general tonics.

Terpene Hydrocarbons are antiviral and contain constituents, such as limonene, pinene and sebanine.

Thujone is toxic, can be irritating and upsetting to the central nervous system. It may be inhaled to relieve respiratory distress and may stimulate the immune system.

Thymol is strongly antiseptic, but not as caustic as phenol.

Oils For Emotional Application

Abuse

> **Blends:** SARA, Hope, Joy, Peace & Calming, Inner Child, Grounding.
> **Single Oils:** Geranium, ylang ylang, sandalwood.

Agitation

> **Blends:** Peace & Calming, Joy, Valor, Harmony, Forgiveness.
> **Single Oils:** Bergamot, cedarwood, clary sage, frankincense, geranium, juniper berry, lavender, myrrh, marjoram, rosewood, rose, ylang ylang, sandalwood.

Anger

> **Blends:** Release, Valor, Sacred Mountain, Joy, Harmony, Hope, Forgiveness, Present Time, Humility.
> **Single Oils:** Bergamot, cedarwood, Roman chamomile, frankincense, lavender, lemon, mandarin, marjoram, melissa, myrrh, orange,rose, petitgraine, sandalwood, ylang ylang.

Apathy

> **Blends:** Joy, Harmony, Valor, 3 Wise Men, Hope, White Angelica.
> **Single Oils:** Frankincense, geranium, marjoram, jasmine, orange, peppermint, rosewood, rose, sandalwood, thyme, ylang ylang.

Argumentative

> **Blends:** Peace & Calming, Joy, Harmony, Hope, Valor, Acceptance, Humility.
> **Single Oils:** Cedarwood, Roman chamomile, eucalyptus, frankincense, jasmine, orange, thyme, ylang ylang.

Boredom

Blends: Dream Catcher, Motivation, Valor, Awaken, Gathering.

Single Oils: Cedarwood, spruce, Roman chamomile, cypress, frankincense, juniper berry, lavender, fir, rosemary, sandalwood, thyme, ylang ylang, pepper.

Confusion

Blends: Clarity, Harmony, Valor, Present Time, Awaken, Gathering.

Single Oils: Cedarwood, spruce, fir, cypress, peppermint, frankincense, geranium, ginger, juniper berry, marjoram, jasmine, rose, rosewood, rosemary, basil, sandalwood, thyme, ylang ylang.

Day Dreaming

Blends: Sacred Mountain, Gathering, Valor, Harmony, Present Time, Dream Catcher, 3 Wise Men.

Single Oils: Eucalyptus, ginger, spruce, lavender, helichrysum, lemon, myrrh, peppermint, rosewood, rose, rosemary, sandalwood, thyme, ylang ylang.

Despair

Blends: Joy, Valor, Harmony, Hope, Gathering, Grounding, Forgiveness, Motivation.

Single Oils: Cedarwood, spruce, fir, clary sage, frankincense, lavender, geranium, lemon, orange, lemongrass, peppermint, spearmint, rosemary, sandalwood, thyme, ylang ylang.

Despondency

Blends: Peace & Calming, Inspiration, Harmony, Valor, Hope, Joy, Present Time, Gathering, Inner Child.

Single Oils: Bergamot, clary sage, cypress, geranium, ginger, orange, rose, rosewood, sandalwood, ylang ylang.

Disappointment

Blends: Hope, Joy, Valor, Present Time, Grounding, Harmony, Dream Catcher, Gathering.

Single Oils: Clary sage, eucalyptus, frankincense, geranium, ginger, juniper berry, lavender, spruce, fir, orange, thyme, ylang ylang.

Discouragement

Blends: Valor, Sacred Mountain, Hope, Joy, Dream Catcher.

Single Oils: Bergamot, cedarwood, frankincense, geranium, juniper berry, lavender, lemon, orange, spruce, rosewood, sandalwood.

Fear

Blends: Valor, Present Time, Hope, White Angelica.

Single Oils: Bergamot, clary sage, Roman chamomile, cypress, geranium, juniper berry, marjoram, myrrh, spruce, fir, orange, sandalwood, rose, ylang ylang.

Forgetfulness

Blends: Clarity, Valor, Present Time, Gathering, 3 Wise Men, Dream Catcher, Acceptance.

Single Oils: Cedarwood, Roman chamomile, eucalyptus, frankincense, rosemary, basil, sandalwood, peppermint, thyme, ylang ylang.

Frustration

Blends: Valor, Hope, Present Time, Sacred Mountain, 3 Wise Men, Humility.

Single Oils: Roman chamomile, clary sage, frankincense, ginger, juniper berry, lavender, lemon, orange, peppermint, thyme, ylang ylang, spruce.

Grief/Sorrow

Blends: Forgiveness, Valor, Joy, Hope, Present Time, White Angelica, Release.

Single Oils: Bergamot, Roman chamomile, clary sage, eucalyptus, juniper berry, lavender.

Guilt

Blends: Valor, Release, Inspiration, Inner child, Gathering, Harmony, Present Time.

Single Oils: Roman chamomile, cypress, juniper berry, lemon, marjoram, geranium, frankincense, spruce, rose, thyme.

Irritability

Blends: Valor, Hope, Forgiveness, Present Time, Inspiration, Humility.

Single Oils: All oils except eucalyptus, peppermint, pepper, and rosemary.

Jealousy

Blends: Valor, Sacred Mountain, White Angelica, Joy, Harmony, Humility, Forgiveness.

Single Oils: Bergamot, eucalyptus, frankincense, lemon, marjoram, orange, rose, rosemary, thyme.

Mood Swings

Blends: Peace & Calming, Gathering, Valor, Dragon Time, Mister, Harmony, Joy, Present Time.

Single Oils: Bergamot, clary sage, sage, geranium, juniper berry, fennel, lavender, lemon, peppermint, rose, jasmine, rosemary, sandalwood, spruce, yarrow, ylang ylang.

Obsessiveness

Blends: Sacred Mountain, Valor, Forgiveness, Acceptance, Humility, Inner Child, Present Time, Awaken, Motivation.

Single Oils: Clary sage, cypress, geranium, lavender, marjoram, rose, sandalwood, ylang ylang, helichrysum.

Panic

Blends: Harmony, Valor, Gathering, White Angelica, Awaken.

Single Oils: Bergamot, Roman chamomile, frankincense, lavender, marjoram, birch, myrrh, rosemary, sandalwood, thyme, ylang ylang, spruce, fir.

Poor Concentration

Blends: Clarity, Awaken, Gathering, Dream Catcher, 3 Wise Men.

Single Oils: Cedarwood, cypress, eucalyptus, juniper berry, lavender, lemon, basil, helichrysum, myrrh, orange, peppermint, rosemary, sandalwood, ylang ylang.

Resentment

Blends: Forgiveness, Harmony, Humility, White Angelica, Release.

Single Oils: Jasmine, rose, tansy.

Restlessness

Blends: Peace & Calming, Sacred Mountain, Gathering, Valor, Harmony, Inspiration, Acceptance, Joy.

Single Oils: Angelica, bergamot, cedarwood, basil, frankincense, geranium, lavender, orange, rose, rosewood, ylang ylang, spruce.

Shock

Blends: Clarity, Valor, Inspiration, Joy, Grounding, Gathering.

Single Oils: Helichrysum, basil, Roman chamomile, myrrh, ylang ylang, rosemary.

Young Living Oil Formulations (Blends)

Most formulas may be applied neat or in dilution with the **V-6 Mixing Oil.** Generally, it is your choice as to how you would like to use them. They may be diffused, applied topically, or added to water for bathing, cleaning and disinfecting. Most oils may be worn as a perfume, aftershave, on the neck, the face, the throat, the wrists, the ankles, the back, behind the ears, over the heart, and, of course, on the bottom of the feet.

Diffusing is always desirable, unless otherwise stated. If you have a double diffuser, you may diffuse two singles, two blends, one single and one blend. You may add single oils to a blend, but do not mix the blends. They are already mixed, and by so doing, you may alter the fragrance and change the desired results. Oils are not to be taken internally; however, you may wish to use a few oils for food flavoring, such as peppermint and lemon.

You may apply one oil or blend after the other. However, if you are using oils for the first time, only use two or three at a time until you see how your body is going to respond. Oils encourage the cells to detoxify, and many people would rather do that slowly.

For an explanation of individual oil characteristics, please refer to the single oil reference guide.

When applying to any area other than Vita Flex points on the feet, use only 1-2 drops.

Abundance

Abundance was created to enhance the frequency of the magnetic field around us through electrical stimulation of the somatides and the cells. This frequency creates the law of attraction.

Diffuse, wear on wrists, behind ears, on neck like perfume, or carry in purse or pocket.

Acceptance

Acceptance stimulates the mind, compelling it to open and accept new things in life that would allow one to reach toward one's higher potential. It also helps one overcome procrastination and denial.

Diffuse, apply over the heart, on the wrists, the neck and the face.

Aroma Life

This may help support cardiovascular function and bring balance to the blood and the lymphatic and circulatory systems.

Apply over the heart, on the feet, on the hand under the ring finger, above the elbow, behind the ring toe on the left foot, and dilute with V-6 Mixing Oil for body massage.

Aroma Siez

This special Blend of essential oils may help relax, calm and relieve tight, sore, tired, and aching muscles resulting from sports injuries, fatigue and stress.

Apply on location for all muscles, neck, feet and stress headaches. Add to bath water and dilute with V-6 Mixing Oil for body massage.

Awaken

This is created from a combination of other Blends. It helps balance one's state of mind and emotions through self-adjustment by allowing a gentle change toward renewal and balance. It awakens one to inner knowing in order to make changes, enabling one to make desirable transitions and reach one's highest potential.

Diffuse, add to bath water, dilute with V-6 Mixing Oil for body massage, wear over the heart, on the wrists, on the neck, and use as an aftershave.

Christmas Spirit

This Blend contains the oils of the evergreens and spices, reminiscent of Christmas, bringing joy, happiness and security.

Diffuse, sprinkle on logs in fireplace, on Christmas trees, on cedar chips for dresser drawers or on potpourri. Use all year round.

Citrus Fresh

This Blend helps bring about a sense of well-being and is said to bring joy to the heart. It has been found to be relaxing and calming, especially for children. It works well as an antiseptic in the air for killing bacteria.

Diffuse, put in bath water, over the heart, on the wrists and the ears, and dilute with V-6 Mixing Oil for full body massage.

Clarity

This Blend has been reported to be beneficial for memory retention and mental alertness. Rosemary and peppermint, found in this Blend, have been used for years to improve energy levels. Dr. Dembar of the University of Cincinnati discovered in his research that inhaling peppermint oil increased the mental accuracy of the students tested by 28 percent.

Diffuse, put in bath water, on cotton ball in air vents, or wear on temples, wrists, neck, etc.

Di-Tone

The oils of tarragon, ginger, peppermint, patchouly, and fennel, found in this Blend, have been reported to assist in relieving digestive irregularity and disturbances, such as an upset stomach, belching and bloating. This Blend is a great companion to ComforTone and JuvaTone.

Apply topically over the stomach or feet and in a compress on the abdomen.

Dragon Time

The oils of clary sage, fennel, marjoram, and lavender, found in this blend, help alleviate those uncomfortable days of the month, reducing cramping and discomfort.

Rub over lower back region, apply on vita flex points on the ankles, use in a compress on the abdomen, and dilute with V-6 Mixing Oil for full body massage.

Dream Catcher

This is an exotic formula of sandalwood, tansanea and spruce, which may enhance dreams and visualization, promoting greater potential for realizing your dreams and staying on your path. It also protects you from negative dreams that might cloud your vision.

Diffuse, apply on forehead, ears, throat, eyebrow, and base of the neck.

Endo Flex

This may help overall endocrine balance, and may support and improve vitality of the body. Sage is traditionally known for assisting with hormonal balance for alleviating hot flashes, myrtle is known for thyroid support, and spearmint is known for balancing metabolism and stimulating weight loss.

Apply over lower back, thyroid, kidneys, liver, feet, and all gland areas.

En-R-Gee

Traditionally, the oils found in this Blend were used for increasing energy in the body. They may help increase circulation and mental alertness.

Diffuse, put on ears, back of neck, put a couple of drops on a cotton ball and place in the air vent of the car, and dilute with V-6 Mixing Oil for full body massage.

Forgiveness

Forgiveness may help release negative memories through the electrical frequencies of the oils, such as frankincense, sandalwood, melissa, etc., found in this Blend.

Apply around navel or wear as a perfume.

Gathering

This was created out of the need to help us overcome the bombardment of chaotic frequencies that alter our focus and take us off our path of higher achievements. Galbanum, a favorite oil of Moses, has a strong effect when blended with frankincense and sandalwood in gathering our emotional and spiritual thoughts. It helps us to focus and hold to the "iron rod," which will enable us to achieve our highest potential.

Diffuse, wear on temples, neck, wrists, etc.

Gentle Baby

This is a beautiful combination for mothers and babies. It is comforting, soothing, and relaxing; and may be beneficial during the birthing process as well as helping to relieve stress during pregnancy. Some of the oil ingredients, such as rose, geranium, ylang ylang and chamomile, are used in European cosmetics to retard wrinkles and enhance the youthful appearance of the skin.

Diffuse, apply over mother's abdomen, on feet, lower back, face and neck areas. Dilute with V-6 Mixing Oil for full body massage, and for applying on baby's skin.

Grounding

We disconnect from reality either because we are excited about new ideas, or because we want to escape into a protective fantasy. When this happens, it is easy to make choices that lead to unfortunate circumstances, such as bad relationships and bad business decisions. We escape because we do not have anchoring or awareness to know how to deal with the emotions. This formula helps stabilize and ground us in order to deal logically with reality in a peaceful manner.

Diffuse, wear on back of neck and on temples.

Harmony

This is an exquisite Blend of 12 oils, including neroli, rose and angelica, promoting physical and emotional healing by bringing about a harmonic balance to the energy centers of the body, allowing the energy to flow more efficiently through the body. It is also beneficial in reducing stress and creating a general overall feeling of well-being.

Diffuse, wear on ears, feet, over the heart, on areas of poor circulation, and over energy centers of the body.

Hope

Everyone needs hope in order to go forward in life. Hopelessness can cause a loss of vision of goals and dreams. This Blend helps to reconnect with a feeling of strength and grounding, restoring hope for tomorrow and helping us to go forward. It may also help overcome suicidal depression.

Diffuse, massage on outer edge of the ears.

Humility

Having humility and forgiveness help us to heal ourselves and our earth (Chronicles 7:14). Humility is an integral ingredient in having forgiveness and seeking a closer relationship with God. Through its frequency and fragrance, you may find that special place where your own healing may begin.

Diffuse, rub over the heart, on neck, temples, etc.

ImmuPower

This oil Blend is for building, strengthening and protecting the body and supporting its defense mechanism.

Diffuse daily to protect your home environment, especially during flu and cold seasons. It may also be applied on the bottom of the feet and along the spine.

Inner Child

This is created for those suffering from abuse. When children have been abused and misused, they become disconnected from their inner child, or identity, which causes confusion. This can contribute to multiple personalties. Sometimes these problems do not manifest themselves until early- to mid-adult years, often labeled as a mid-life crisis. This fragrance may stimulate memory response and help one reconnect with the inner-self or one's identity. This is one of the first steps to finding emotional balance.

Apply around navel and nose.

Inspiration

This is a combination of oils traditionally used by the Eastern and North American natives to increase spirituality, enhancing prayer and inner awareness.

Diffuse, wear on forehead and back of neck.

Into The Future

This helps one leave the past behind in order to go forward with vision and excitement. So many times we find ourselves settling for mediocrity and sacrificing one's own potential and success because of the fear of the unknown and what the future may or may not hold. This Blend was formulated to support the emotions in helping us create the feeling of moving forward and not being afraid to let determination and that pioneering spirit come through. Living on the edge with tenacity and integrity brings the excitement of the challenge and the joy of success.

Diffuse, put in bath water, over the heart, on wrists, neck, as a compress, and dilute with V-6 Mixing Oil for full body massage.

Joy

Joy produces a magnetic energy to enhance the frequency of self-love and bring joy to the heart. It has been very helpful in overcoming grief.

Diffuse, put in bath water, over the heart, on wrists, neck, as a compress, and dilute with V-6 Mixing Oil for full body massage.

Juva Flex

This formulation is a combination of oils that have been known to support liver and lymphatic system detoxification as well as support digestion.

Apply over liver, on Vita Flex points on the feet, and on the spine.

Melrose

This Blend has antiseptic-like properties when used topically for cleansing cuts, scrapes, burns, rashes and bruised tissue. It may also help prevent growth of bacteria, fungus or infection.

Diffuse to dispel odors, apply topically on cuts, scrapes, burns, rashes, and any infection.

Mister

This may help to decongest the prostate and promote greater hormonal balance. Some women have found it to reduce hot flashes.

Apply around ankles and prostate for men.

Motivation

This has an electrical frequency, which may help enable one to overcome the feelings of fear and procrastination, and help stimulate feelings of moving forward and accomplishing new things.

Diffuse, apply on ears, feet (big toe), on chest or the nap of the neck.

My-Grain

This contains oils that were traditionally used to relieve headaches, nausea, depression and problems related to severe migraine headaches.

Place two drops in the palm of the hands and cup over the nose and inhale. Put on temples, forehead, and back of neck.

Pane Away

It helps to reduce inflammation, promoting healthy circulation and healing, thus reducing pain. Many people have had relief from arthritis symptoms, sports injuries, sprains, muscle spasms, bumps and bruises.

Apply on location for muscles, cramps, bruises, compress on the spine and Vita Flex points on the feet.

Peace & Calming

This Blend promotes relaxation and a sense of peace after a stressful day. When diffused in the home, it may help calm overactive and hard-to-manage children.

Diffuse, wear as a perfume, apply on bottom of the feet.

Present Time

This empowering fragrance gives a feeling of being "in the moment." One can only go forward and progress when in the present time.

Rub on sternum, neck, and forehead. It is also wonderful as an aftershave mixed with Pharaoh lotion.

Purification

This Blend helps to purify the air in the home and work environment. It neutralizes mildew, cigarette smoke, poison from insect bites, such as spiders, bees, hornets, wasps, and other noxious odors found in homes, offices and other confined areas.

Diffuse, apply topically to disinfect, put on cotton balls to place in air vents of home, car, hotel room, office, etc. It has been said to repel bugs, insects, and mice.

Raven

This combination of ravensara and eucalyptus radiata, gives strength in fighting respiratory disease and infections; and may help alleviate symptoms of tuberculosis, asthma and pneumonia.

Diffuse, apply topically over lungs and throat, put on pillow at night, use in a suppository application with V-6 Mixing Oil.

R.C.

This Blend was formulated to help give relief from colds, bronchitis, sinusitis and respiratory congestion. Diffusing may help decongest and relieve allergy-type symptoms, such as coughs and sore throats.

Diffuse, apply on chest, neck, ears, bottom of feet, and can be used in a humidifier.

Release

This may stimulate a sense of harmony and balance within the mind and body; and help release anger and frustration to bring about a sense of peace and emotional well-being.

Apply directly over the liver, or as a compress, on the bottom of the feet, and behind the ears.

Relieve It

This has oils which contain high anti-inflammatory action for the benefit of relieving deep tissue pain.

Apply on location anywhere for pain.

Sacred Mountain

This is a Blend of oils that are extracted from conifers, such as fir, spruce and pine, and represent the sacred feeling of the mountains. They have been reported to bring about a feeling of protection, strength and security.

Diffuse, put on crown of head, wrists and behind ears.

SARA

This has a fragrance that, when inhaled may enable one to relax into a mental state whereby one may be able to release and let go of the memory trauma of Sexual And/or Ritual Abuse.

Apply over energy centers, on Vita Flex points, temples and nose.

Sensation

This has the beautiful fragrance of ylang ylang, rose, and jasmine, which is extremely uplifting, refreshing and arousing. Sensation is also very beneficial for skin problems of any kind.

Apply on location, use for massage and add to your sensation bath and shower gel.

Thieves

This was created from research about the thieves during the 16th century plague in England who rubbed oils all over their bodies to protect themselves while they were robbing the dead and dying. The assumption was that these oils strengthened the immune system, thus protecting them from disease.

Diffuse periodically for one-half hour at a time in the work or home environment. It may be applied to the bottom of the feet or diluted with V-6 Mixing Oil for massage under arms to stimulate the lymphatics, and on the thymus to stimulate the immune system.

3 Wise Men

This Blend was formulated to open the subconscious mind through pineal stimulation in order to release deep-seated trauma encoded in the DNA of the cells. The oils bring a sense of grounding and uplifting through emotional releasing, and elevate spiritual consciousness.

Put a couple of drops on the crown of the head, eyebrow, solar plexes, and thymus. It may also be diffused.

Valor

This Blend helps balance electrical energies within the body, giving courage, confidence and self-esteem. It has been found to help the body self-correct its physical and structural alignment.

Diffuse, apply on bottom of feet, on throat, wrists, solar plexes, and over thymus.

White Angelica

This is a combination of 18 oils, some of which were used during ancient times to increase the aura around the body. It brings a delicate sense of strength and protection, creating a feeling of wholeness in the realm of one's own spirituality. Its frequency protects against the bombardment of negative energy.

Diffuse, wear on top of shoulders, on crown, wrists, behind ears, and is excellent for a bath.

Young Living Single Oils

The following is a list of the single oils sold by Young Living or used in Young Living Essential Oil formulations. Some of the main chemical constituents have been listed to help you understand their usage. Please refer to the pages on constituents for an explanation.

Angelica *(Angelica archangelica)*
Constituents: Monoterpenes (73%): Pinenes, limonene (13%); Esters: bornyle acetates; Coumarines (2%).

This oil is referred to by the German people as the "oil of angels." It has been incredible in bringing the memory back to the point of origin before trauma or anger was experienced. It helps one to release and let go of negative feelings. It is sedative, anticoagulant, and calming.

Basil *(Ocimum Basilicum)*
Constituents: Monoterpenes (5%): pinenes; Sesquiterpene (10%); Mono-terpenols: linalol, terpineol; Methyl-ether phenols: (75-85%): methyl carvacol (22-25%), eugenol (55-60%).

This oil has been found to be beneficial for alleviating mental fatigue, spasms, rhinitis, and as a first aid treatment for wasp stings and snake bites. It may also help when there is a loss of smell due to chronic nasal catarrh.

Bergamot *(Citrus Aurantium Bergamia)*

Constituents: Aldehydes: Citrals (45%); Furocoumarines.

This oil has been used in the Middle East for hundreds of years for acne, boils, cold sores, eczema, insect bites, insect repellent, oily complexion, psoriasis, scabies, spot varicose veins, ulcers, wounds, sore throat, thrush, infectious disease, and depression. It is known to have about 300 chemical constituents, and has a refreshing, uplifting quality.

Birch *(Betula Alleghaniensis)*

Constituents: Esters: methyl salicylate (99%).

This oil is beneficial for bone, muscle and joint discomfort. It contains 99 percent methyl salicylate, which has a cortisone-like action. It has been helpful in decreasing pain from arthritis, tendonitis, and rheumatism.

Black Cumin *(Cuminum Cyminum)*

Constituents: Monoterpenes (30-60%): pinen (13-22%), paracymene (3-9%), terpinene (12-32%); Coumarines.

This oil, commonly found in Egypt, helps with digestion and supports the immune system. It is usually kept on the dinner table and used for food flavoring during meal time. It is antiseptic, antispasmodic, and carminative.

Cassia (*Cinnamomum Cassia*)

Constituents: Phenols; Aldehydes (78-88%); Coumarines.

This oil is anti-infectious, antibacterial, and anti-coagulant.

Cedarwood *(Cedrus Atlantica)*

Constituents: Sesquiterpenes (50%); Sesquiterpenols (30%); Sesquiter-penones (20%).

This oil is historically recognized for its purifying properties, and is used in avoiding hair loss, dandruff, acne, psoriasis, arthritis, congestion, coughs, sinusitis, cystitis and nervous tension.

Chamomile, German *(Maticaria Recutita)*

Constituents: Sesquiterpenes; Sesquiterpenols; Sesquiterpene Oxides; Coumarines; Esters.

This has been a highly respected oil for over 3,000 years and has been used for helping skin conditions, such as dermatitis, boils, acne, rashes, and eczema. It is also used for hair care, burns, cuts, toothaches, teething pains, inflamed joints, menopausal problems, insomnia, migraine headaches and stress-related complaints.

Chamomile, Roman *(Chamaemelum Nobile)*

Constituents: Esters (75-80%), d'isobutyle (36-40%), cetones (13%).

This oil may help with restless legs, insomnia, muscle tension, cuts, scrapes, bruises and is anti-infectious. It is used extensively in Europe for the skin.

Cinnamon Bark *(Cinnamomum Verum)*

Constituents: Aromatic alcohols; Esters; Phenols; Aldehydes: cinnamaldehyde (63-76%); Coumarines.

Sri-Lanka has been producing this oil for over 2,000 years. It is used in the Middle East and Orient for fighting viruses and infectious disease. Dr. J. C. Lapraz found that viruses could not live in the presence of cinnamon oil. Because of its high phenol content, it is best diluted before being applied on the skin.

Cistus *(Cistus Ladaniferus)*

Constituents: Monoterpenes: pinene (50%), camphene (4%); Monoterpene alcohols; Esters: linalyle acetates; Phenols: eugenol (1%), thymol; Aldehydes; Cetones.

This oil is high in phenols, which support and strengthen the autoimmune and immune systems.

Citronella *(Cymbopogon Nardus)*

Constituents: Terpene alcohols (35%): geraniol (18%), borneol (6%), citronnellol (8%); Aldehydes (5-15%): citronnellal (5%); Esters (9%); Phenols (9%): methyl isoeugenol (7%).

This oil is antiseptic, antibacterial, antispasmodic, anti-inflammatory, and insecticidal.

Clary Sage *(Salvia Sclarea)*

Constituents: In this oil there are 250 plus constituents. Monoterpenes: pinenes, camphene, limonene, terpinolene; Sesquiterpenes; Terpene alcohols; Monoterpenols (15%): linalol (6-16%), terpinene, citronnellol, nerol, geraniol, borneol, thujol; Esters (75%): linalyle acetate (62-75%); Oxides; Cetones; Aldehydes; Coumarines.

This oil is beneficial in regulating cells and balancing hormones. It helps with circulatory problems and hemorrhoids.

Clove *(Eugenia Caryophyllus)*

Constituents: Sesquiterpenes; Esters: eugenyle (22%), terpenyle; Phenols: eugenol (70-80%); Oxides.

It is anti-infectious, antibacterial, antiviral, antifungal, antiparasitic, and antiseptic. It is used in European hospitals for dental infections, viral hepatitis, bacterial colitis, cholera, amoebic dysentery, infectious acne, nervites, cystites, sinusitis, bronchitis, flu, tuberculosis, hypertension, thyroid dysfunction, and fatigue.

Coriander *(Coriandrum Sativum)*

Constituents: Aldehydes (85-95%), 7-dodecanal (21%).

This oil, as shown in research from Cairo University, lowers glucose levels by normalizing insulin levels and supporting pancreas function. It also has anti-inflammatory and sedative properties.

Cypress *(Cupressus Sempervirens)*

Constituents: Monoterpenes: pinenes (45%); Sesquiterpenes; Sesquiterpenols.

This oil is beneficial for decongesting the circulatory and lymphatic systems, and may help with edema, cellulite, varicose veins and water retention. It is anti-infectious, antibacterial, and antimicrobial.

Davana *(Artemisa Pallens)*

Constituents: Sesquiterpenones (36-54%): (+) davanone (25-52%); Diéthers.

This oil is anti-infectious, soothing to rough, dry and chapped skin, and stimulating to the endocrine system, perhaps improving hormonal balance. It has also been known to help with painful scarring, excess gas and spasms.

Dill *(Anethum Graveolens)*

Constituents: Monoterpenes (25-50%): (+) - limonenes (25-40%), α-phellandrene (25%), Monoterpenones (40-60%), Coumarines (4%).

This oil has been proven, through research at Cairo University, to help lower glucose levels by normalizing insulin levels and supporting pancreas function. In European hospitals it is also used for bronchial catarrh and liver deficiencies

Eucalyptus *(Eucalyptus Globulus)*

Constituents: Monoterpenes; Sesquiterpenes; Monoterpene alcohols; Sesquiterpenols; Oxides: cineole (70-75%); Aldehydes.

This is a powerful herb when dealing with viruses of the respiratory system. It is anticatarrhal, expectorant, mucolytic, antibacterial, antifungal, antiviral, and antiseptic.

Eucalyptus *(Eucalyptus Radiata)*

Constituents: Monoterpenes; Monoterpenols (20%); Terpene oxides: cineole (62-72%).

This is anti-inflammatory, anti-infectious, antibacterial, antiviral, anticatarrhal, and expectorant. It has been known to help with inflammation of the nasal mucous membrane, as well as with nasal nasopharynx, flu, inflammation of the ear, sinusitis, bronchitis, hay fever, inflammation of the iris, vaginitis, endometriosis, and acne.

Fennel *(Foeniculum Vulgare)*

Constituents: Monoterpenes: limonene (18-29%); Monoterpenols: fenchol; Phenols: methyl chavicol; Aldyhydes; Cetones: camphor; Oxides: cineole: Coumarines; Furocoumarines.

This oil is antispasmodic, antiseptic, and stimulating to the cardiovascular and respiratory systems. With its hormone-like activity, it may help facilitate delivery and increase the production of milk.

Fir *(Abies Alba)*

Constituents: Monoterpenes (90-95%): pinenes (24%), camphene (21%), limonene (34%); Esters (5-10%): bornyle acetate.

This oil has traditionally been used to help support the body and reduce the symptoms of arthritis, rheumatism, bronchitis, coughs, sinusitis, colds, flu and fevers. It has been found to be beneficial in fighting airborne germs and bacteria. It is antiseptic, anticatarrhal, antiarthritic, and stimulating.

Frankincense *(Boswellia Carterii)*

Constituents: Monoterpenes (40%): pinene, limonene; Sesquiterpenes: gurjunene; Terpenes alcohols.

This is known as the "holy oil" in the Middle East, and was used religiously for thousands of years. It was well known for its healing powers during the time of Christ. It is now being researched and used therapeutically in European hospitals. It is anticatarrhal, prevents scarring, antitumoral, immune-stimulating, and antidepressant. It is stimulating and elevating to the mind, and helps in overcoming depression.

Galbanum *(Ferula Gummose)*

Constituents: Monoterpernes (65-85%), pinene (45-50%), carene (10-20%); Sesquiterpenols: guaiol, bulsenol, galbanol; Esters; Coumarines.

This favorite oil of Moses, written about in the book of *Exodus,* was used for both medicinal and spiritual purposes. It is recognized for its antiviral properties and overall body strength and supporting properties. Alone, its frequency is low; but when combined with other oils, such as frankincense or sandalwood, the frequency increases dramatically.

Geranium *(Pelargonium x asperum)*

Constituents: Monoterpenes; Sesquiterpenes; Monoterpenes (60-68%), citronnellol (33%), geraniol (25%); Esters (20-33%); Oxydes; Aldehydes; Cetones.

This oil has been used for centuries for skin care. Its strength lies in the ability to regenerate tissue and nerves and to assist in balancing hormonal problems. It is excellent for the skin of expectant mothers, and its aromatic influence helps release negative memories. In Europe it is also used as an antispasmotic, relaxant, anti-inflammatory, liver and pancreas stimulant and is anti-infectious, antibacterial and antifungal. It may also help with nervous colitis, plaque, ulcerations, fungus, hemorrhoids, and anxiety.

Ginger *(Zingiber Officinale)*

Constituents: Monoterpenes: pinenes, camphene; Sesquiterpenes; Hydrocarbons; Monoterpene alcohols: linalol; Sesquiterpene alcohols.

Ginger has been used in the East for thousands of years. It is used for relief from arthritis, rheumatism, sprains, muscular aches and pains, catarrh, congestion, coughs, sinusitis, sore throats, diarrhea, colic, cramps, indigestion, loss of appetite, motion sickness, fever, flu, chills, and infectious disease.

Grapefruit *(Citrus Paradisii)*

Constituents: Monoterpenes: limonene (96%); Aldehydes; Coumarines; Furocoumarines.

This oil may be beneficial for digestive complaints, obesity, reducing water retention and cellulite. It also works well as a disinfectant.

Helichrysum *(Helichrysum Italicum)*

Constituents: Sesquiterpenes: caryophyllene; Monoterpenes: nerol; Terpene esters: neryl acetate (75%); Cetones (15-20%).

European researchers have found that this oil regenerates tissue, reduces tissue pain and may help to improve skin conditions and circulatory function. It is anticoagulant, prevents phlebitis, helps regulate cholesterol, stimulates liver cell function, is anticatarrhal, mucolytic, expectorant, antispasmodic, and reduces scarring and discoloration. In 1991, I discovered the pain-reducing benefits of helichrysum and in 1992 discovered its benefits in helping to improve certain hearing losses.

Hyssop *(Hyssopus Officinalis)*

Constituents: Monoterpenes (25-30%): pinene (15-22%); Sesquiterpenes (12%); Phenols; Monoterpenones (45-58%), isopinocamphone (31-32%), pinocamphone (53%).

Hyssop was used by Moses because of its anti-inflammatory and antiviral properties. It opens the respiratory system and discharges toxins and mucous. It is anticatarrhal, mucolytic, decongestant, antiasthmatic, anti-infectious, antiparasitic, anti-inflammatory of the pulmonary, regulates lipid metabolism and prevents scarring.

Jasmine *(Jasminum Officinale)*

Constituents: Benzyl benzoate acetate.

Jasmine is beneficial for the skin, reducing problems such as dry, greasy, irritated or sensitive skin. It is also used for muscle spasms, sprains, catarrh, coughs, hoarseness, laryngitis, uterine disorder, labor pains, frigidity, depression and nervous exhaustion.

Juniper Berry *(Juniperus Communis)*

Constituents: Monoterpenes: pinene (34-46%), sabinene (9-28%), mycrene (6-8%); Sesquiterpenes; Terpenes alcohols (5-10%); Aldyhydes; Cetones.

This oil may work as a detoxifier and cleanser, reducing dermatitis, eczema and acne. It has also been used to promote better nerve and kidney function.

Lavender *(Lavandula Officinalis)*

Constituents: Monoterpenes; Sesquiterpenes; Non terpene alcohols (45%); Esters: linalyle acetate (42-45%); coumarines.

Lavender is known as the universal oil, and may be beneficial for skin conditions, such as burns, rashes, and psoriasis, and may also help with insomnia. It is antispasmodic, sedative, hypotensive, calming, anti-inflammatory, analgesic, anti-infectious, cardiotonic, and anticoagulant. It prevents scarring and relieves headaches and P.M.S. symptoms.

Lemon *(Citrus Limon)*

Constituents: Monoterpenes: limonene (54-72%), terpinenes (7-14%); Sesquiterpenes; Aldehydes; Coumarines.

Lemon has been found to promote leukocyte formation, dissolve cellulite, increase lymphatic function, and promote a sense of well-being. It is also beneficial for the skin, serves in the purification of air and water, and works well in removing gum, oil and grease spots.

Lemongrass *(Cymbopogon Flexuosus)*

Constituents: Monoterpene alcohols; Sesquiterpene alcohols: farnesol (12%); Monoterpene aldehydes (60-85%): citrals (75%), neral (27%), geranial (46%).

This oil works well for purification. It may be beneficial for the digestive system, and has been reported to help regenerate connective tissue. It is a vasodilator, anti-inflammatory, sedative and supportive to the digestive system.

Mandarin *(Citrus Reticulata)*

Constituents: Monoterpenes: limonene (65-94%); Monoterpenols; Esters; Aldehydes; Coumarines.

This oil is appeasing, gentle, helps with insomnia and promotes happiness. It is antispasmodic, antiseptic, antifungal, affects hepatic duct function, and works as a digestive tonic.

Marjoram *(Origanum Majorana)*

Constituents: Monoterpenes (40%); Sesquiterpenes; Monoterpenols (50%); Esters: terpenyle acetates, linalyle acetates.

This oil is calming to the respiratory system and assists in relieving spasms and migraine headaches. It is anti-infectious, antibacterial, antiseptic, soothing to the nerves, and may work as a diuretic.

Melaleuca *(Melaleuca Alternifolia)*

Constituents: Monoterpenes: paracymene (3-20%); Monoterpene alcohols (45-50%): terpinene (25-45%).

This species is anti-infectious, antibacterial, antifungal, antiviral, antiparasitic, antiseptic, anti-inflammatory, immune-stimulating, decongestant, neurotonic, and analgesic.

Melaleuca *(Melaleuca Quienervia)*

Constituents: Sesquiterpenes; Sesquiterpene alcohols: trans-nerolidol (81-82%); Terpene oxides.

This species is antifungal, antibacterial, antiseptic, anti-inflammatory, a digestive tonic and a strong tissue regenerator.

Melissa *(Melissa Officinalis)*

Constituents: Monoterpenes; Monoterpenols: linalol, nerol, geraniol, citronnellol; Sesquiterpenols; Esters; Terpene oxides; Monoterpenals: citrals, neral (15%), geranial (15%).

This oil has powerful antiviral constituents. It is very gentle and delicate because of the nature of the plant, and helps to bring out those characteristics within the individual.

Mountain Savory *(Satureja Montana)*

Constituents: Monoterpenes: thujene, pinenes, camphene, terpinenes (20%); Sesquiterpenes; Esters; Phenols: thymol, carvacrol (25-50%), eugenol; Cetones.

This oil is antibacterial, antiviral, antifungal, antiparasitic, immune-stimulating and a general tonic for the body.

Myrrh *(Commiphora Molmol)*

Constituents: Sesquiterpenes: (29%); Cetones; Aldehydes.

Myrrh is anti-infectious and supportive to the immune system. The Arabian people found it to be beneficial for skin conditions; such as, athletes foot, chapped and cracked skin, eczema, ringworm, wounds, and wrinkles. It was used to help with asthma, bronchitis, catarrh, coughs, gingivitis (gum infection), mouth ulcers and sore throat. It may also help alleviate diarrhea, dyspepsia, flatulence, and hemorrhoids. It also decongests the prostate and normalizes hyper-thyroid problems.

Myrtle *(Myrtus Communis)*

Constituents: Monoterpenes: pinene (24-25%); Sesquiterpenes; Mono-terpene alcohols, Terpene esters; Terpene oxides: cineole (45%); Aldehydes.

According to Dr. Pénoël, this oil may normalize hormonal imbalances of the thyroid and ovaries as well as balance the hypothyroid. Research has shown it to help the respiratory system with chronic coughs and tuberculosis. It is suitable to use for coughs and chest complaints with children, and may help support the immune function in fighting colds, flu and infectious disease.

Neroli *(Citrus Aurantium)*

Constituents: Monoterpenes (35%): pinene (17%), limonene (11%); Terpene alcohols (40%): linalol (30-32%); Terpene esters (6-21%): linalyl acetate (5-7%); Sesquiterpene alcohols (6%); Cetones.

Neroli has been regarded by the Egyptian people for its great attributes for healing the mind, body and spirit. It is antibacterial, antiviral, antiparasitic, anti-infectious, and works well as a support to the digestive system. It brings everything into focus at the moment.

Nutmeg *(Myristica Fragrans)*

Constituents: Monoterpenes: pinenes (15%), mycrene (12%), sabinene (15%), terpenes (8-12%), linonene (4%); Monoterpenols: terpinene (4%); Phenols.

This oil has adrenal cortex-like activity, which helps support the adrenal glands for increased energy. Historically, it has been known to benefit circulation, muscles, joints, arthritis, gout, muscular aches and pains, rheumatism, flatulence, indigestion, sluggish digestion, nausea and helps fight bacterial infection. It also helps to support the nervous system to overcome frigidity, impotence, neuralgia and nervous fatigue.

Orange *(Citrus Aurantium)*

Constituents: Monoterpenes (90-92%): limonene (90%), terpinolene; Esters; Aldehydes; Coumarines.

Orange brings peace and happiness to the mind and body. It has been recognized to help a dull, oily complexion, mouth ulcers, obesity, fluid retention, colds, flu, constipation and dyspepsia.

Oregano *(Origanum Compactum)*

Constituents: Monoterpenes (25%); Sesquiterpenes; Monoterpenols; Monoterpene phenols (60-70%): carvacrol, thymol; Methyl-ester phenols: methyl carvacrol; Cetones.

This oil has powerful antiviral, antibacterial, antifungal and anti-parasitic properties, and may aid in the ability to balance metabolism and strengthen the vital centers of the body.

Palmarosa *(Cymbopogon Martinii)*

Constituents: Monoterpenes; Alcohols: geraniol (35-65%).

This oil helps with skin problems; such as, candida, rashes, scaly and flaky skin. It is antimicrobial, antibacterial, antifungal and antiviral. It is supportive to the nerves and cardiovascular systems.

Patchouly *(Pogostemon Cablin)*

Constituents: Monoterpenes; Sesquiterpenes (40-45%); Sesquiterpenols: patchoulol (35-40%).

Patchouly is very beneficial for the skin, and may help prevent wrinkles or chapped skin. It is a general tonic and stimulant and helps the digestive system. It is also anti-inflammatory, anti-infectious, antiseptic, tissue regenerating, works as a decongestant, and helps relieve itching from hives.

Pepper, Black *(Piper Nigrum)*

Constituents: Monoterpenes (4%); Sesquiterpenes (85-90%); Cetones; Aldehydes.

This oil stimulates the endocrine system and helps increase energy. It is anti-inflammatory, anticatarrhal, expectorant, supportive to the digestive glands, and traditionally used for rheumatoid arthritis. It also increases cellular oxygenation.

Peppermint *(Mentha Piperita)*

Constituents: Monoterpenes (2-18%); Sesquiterpenes; Monoterpenols: menthol (38-48%); Monoterpenones: menthone (20-30% and up to 65%); Terpene oxides: cineole (5%); Terpene esters; Coumarines.

This oil is reported by Dr. Pénoël to help reduce fevers, candida, nausea, vomiting, and to aid in respiratory function. It may be used in water for flavoring, and helps in cooling the body during hot summer days.

Petitgrain *(Citrus Aurantium)*

Constituents: Monoterpenes (10%); Monoterpene Alcohols (30-40%): linalol (20-27%); Ester terpenols (50-70%), linalyle acetate (45-55%).

This oil is antispasmodic, anti-inflammatory, anti-infectious, anti-bacterial, and re-establishes nerve equilibrium.

Ravensara *(Ravensara Aromatica)*

Constituents: Monoterpenes: pinenes (high elevation); Sesquiterpenes; Monoterpenols: terpineol; Ester terpenes: terpene acetate; Terpene oxides: cineole.

This oil is referred to by the people of Madagascar as "the oil that heals" because of its antiseptic activity, as well as its aid in respiratory problems. It is anti-infectious, antiviral, antibacterial, expectorant and supporting to the nerves. It has shown to help with rhinopharyngitis, flu, sinusitis, bronchitis, viral hepatitis, cholera, herpes, infectious mononucleosis, insomnia, and muscle fatigue.

Rose *(Rosa Damascena)*

Constituents: Hydrocarbons; Monoterpenols: geraniol, citronellol, nerol (5%), linalol; Sesquiterpene Alcohols; Esters (2-5%); Phenols; oxides: rose oxides.

Rose has the highest frequency of 320 Hertz. Its beautiful fragrance is almost intoxicating and aphrodisiac-like. It enhances the frequency of every cell, bringing balance and harmony to the body. It is antihemorrhaging, anti-infectious and prevents scarring. Dr. Pénoël states that it may help with chronic bronchitis, asthma, tuberculosis, sexual disabilities, frigidity, impotency, skin disease, wounds, ulcers, sprains, wrinkles, thrush, and gingivitis. It is stimulating and elevating to the mind, creating a sense of well-being.

Rosemary *(Rosmarinus Officinalis)*

Constituents: Monoterpenes: pinene (15-34%); Sesquiterpenes; Monoterpenols: borneol (7%), camphor (1-15%); Oxides.

This oil may be beneficial for skin conditions and dandruff, and may help fight candida and support the immune system. It is anti-catarrhal, anti-infectious, antispasmodic, balances the endocrine system, is an expectorant and helps overcome mental fatigue.

Rosewood *(Aniba Rosaeodora)*

Constituents: Monoterpenols: linalol (95%).

This oil is soothing, creates skin elasticity, and helps the skin rid itself of irritations and problems, such as candida. It is anti-infectious, antibacterial, antifungal, antiviral, and antiparasitic. Our research at Weber State University in October of 1995 has shown this oil to have the highest inhibition rate of all the oils tested against gram positive and gram negative bacterial growth.

Sage *(Salvia Officinalis)*

Constituents: Monoterpenes; Hydrocarbons; Monoterpenols: linalol (5-12 %); Sesquiterpenols; Esters; Phenols: thymol; Oxides: cineol (5-14%); Monoterpenones (20-70%): α-thujone (12-33%), β-thujone (2-14%), camphor (26%); Aldehydes, Coumarines.

It has been used in Europe for skin conditions, such as eczema, acne, dandruff and hair loss. It has been recognized for its benefits of strengthening the vital centers, metabolism and aiding in menopause. It may help in relieving depression and mental fatigue.

Sandalwood *(Santalum Album)*

Constituents: Sesquiterpenes; Sesquiterpenols: α and β-santalols (67%); Sesquiterpenals.

Similar to frankincense, this oil is supporting to the lymphatic, nervous and cardiovascular systems, and relieves the symptoms of sciatica and lumbago. Traditionally, it was used for skin regeneration, yoga, meditation and has been found to help remove negative programming from the cells and increases oxygen around the pituitary and pineal glands.

Spearmint *(Mentha Spicata)*

Constituents: Monoterpenes: camphene, limonene (8-20%), Sesquiterpenes; Monoterpenols; Terpene esters (30-37%): Monoterpenones: carvone (55-65%).

This oil may aid the respiratory, nervous, and glandular systems. It is antispasmodic, anti-infectious, antiparasitic, antiseptic, and anti-inflammatory. Its hormone-like activity may help open and release emotional blocks, and bring about a feeling of balance. It has been used to increase metabolism to burn fat.

Spruce *(Picea Mariana)*

Constituents: Monoterpenes (50-55%): camphene (10-15%), α-pinene (13-16%); Sesquiterpenes; Monoterpenols (+) borneal; Esters (30-37%): (-) bornyle acetate (30-37%); Sesquiterpenols.

This oil may aid the respiratory, nervous and glandular systems. Its aromatic influences help to open and release emotional blocks, bringing about a feeling of balance.

Tangerine *(Citrus Tangerina)*

Constituents: Linolene.

This oil is calming, sedating, anti-inflammatory, anticoagulant, and helps with anxiety, dizziness, and nervousness.

Tarragon *(Artemisia Dracunculus)*

Constituents: Phenols: methyl chavicol (60-75%); Coumarines.

Tarragon has been used in Europe to reduce anorexia, dyspepsia, flatulence, intestinal spasms, nervous digestion, sluggish digestion and genital urinary tract infection. It may also help reduce premenstrual discomfort and pain with nerves and sciatica. It is neuro-muscular, antispasmodic, anti-inflammatory, anti-infectious, antiviral, antibacterial, and prevents fermentation.

Thyme *(Thymus Vulgaris)*

Constituents: Monoterpenols: linalol (60-80%); Terpene esters.

Thyme may be beneficial in supporting immunological functions and overcoming fatigue and physical weakness after illness. It is antimicrobial, antibacterial, antifungal, antiviral and works as a uterotonic, neurotonic, and cardiotonic.

White Lotus *(Nymphaea Lotus)*

This oil was revered as one of the most exotic and treasured flowers in ancient Egypt. It provided the foundation of medicine as it contained anticancerous properties and helped prevent diabetes. Science has done little research on this plant or oil, so there is much yet to learn; but the fragrance is very intoxicating and uplifting to the emotions.

Wild Tansy *(Tanacetum Vulgare)*

Constituents: Monoterpenes; β-thyone (87%); α-thyene; Linalol; Camphene.

This oil has been shown to be very supportive of the immune system. It encourages an uplifting feeling, a positive attitude and a general feeling of well-being. It is antiviral, anti-infectious, antibacterial, fights colds, flu and infections. According to E. Joseph Montagna's P.D.R. on herbal formulas, wild Idaho tansy may help with weak veins, promote suppressed menstruation, improve weakness of the kidneys, tuberculosis, heart disorders, palpitations, sciatica, rheumatism, inflammation, sprains, bruises, freckles, sunburn, toothache, inflamed eyes, colds, flu, gout, dyspepsia, jaundice, stomach sickness, diarrhea, soothes the bowels and tones the entire system.

Ylang Ylang *(Cananga Odorata)*

Constituents: Sesquiterpenes; Monoterpene alcohols: linalol (55%); Esters; Phenols; Methyl ether phenols: methyl cresol (15%).

This oil may be extremely effective in calming and bringing about a sense of relaxation. It is antispasmodic, balances equilibrium, helps with sexual disabilities and frigidity, and has been used traditionally to balance heart function.

Young Living Food Supplements, Tinctures and Teas

Most people in America seem to have digestive problems; such as, constipation, gas, bloating, indigestion, morning sickness, etc. They rub the essential oil formula Di-Tone, which contains peppermint oil, on their stomachs and are surprised that their symptoms go away almost immediately. It is wonderful to know that we don't have to ingest the oils for them to work. I discovered in clinical practice, while doing bacteriology studies with the blood, that there was an incredible amount of food bacteria in the blood serum because it didn't digest and couldn't get through the cell wall because of low oxygen levels. When we put the oils in the food products, we would not find any undigested food bacteria in the blood.

When used as a food additive, essential oils increase the absorption of the food nutrients. In order to have good health, the body must be cleansed of toxins. It is important to cleanse the bowels because from here toxins are released into the blood stream and travel to all parts of the body. It appears that the oils help the food digest better, prevent unfriendly bacteria growth and increase cell metabolism because of their oxygenating molecules. This in turn may help in balancing the pH of the cell for increased nutritional intake while enhancing the delivery of nutrients to the cells. These products provide an easy, gentle way for the body to cleanse itself. To my knowledge, I was the first to incorporate essential oils into food supplements as a flavoring and preserving agent, which has been a very exciting advancement in the field of food supplementation.

A. D. & E.

This is a liquid combination of vitamins A, D and E formulated with the essential oils of spearmint and peppermint. This powerful antioxidant of beta carotene has been reported to help improve eyesight, skin, hair and the immune system.

Arthro Plus

This is an herbal tincture that, combined with essential oils, can be taken orally or topically for help in the relief of arthritic pain, rheumatism, or bursitis. It works well with ArthroTune.

ArthroTune

The ingredients of butcher's broom, yucca, alfalfa leaf and capsicum were all used to fight arthritis. Pure grape pit extract (active OPCs 85+ Proanthocyanidins), Uncaria Tomentosa and alpha gluteric acid make this a powerful formula when used to fight and protect the body against arthritis.

Body Balance

This is a unique product resulting from years of research and is designed to help balance the body at its ideal weight. Advanced technology has made low-heat, glasspack pasteurization of nonfat dry milk possible, leaving the enzymes intact. Lecithin gives the body tissue elasticity and fatty acids required to maintain a proper digestive balance. It contains a complete amino acid and vitamin profile, and has a high level of protein to maintain muscle tissue. The oils in Body Balance may help dissolve hard fatty deposits and decongest the lymphatic system. It may be used as a meal replacement and is delicious blended with fresh fruit or juice.

Chelex

This contains herbal ingredients synergistically formulated to help rid the body of heavy metals and other immune-damaging free radicals. Heavy metals absorbed from the air, water, food, skin care products, etc., lodge and store in the fatty layers of the body and give off toxic gases in the system, which may create allergic symptoms. Ridding our bodies of heavy metals is extremely important in order to have healthy immune function, especially if we have mercury fillings. This formula contains the essential oil of helichrysum, which may help the body in the elimination of heavy metals because of its natural chelating action.

Colloidal Essence

This is a special formulation combining colloidal gold and silver. Colloidal gold has been used to prevent and help overcome arthritis and has exceptional anti-inflammatory properties. Colloidal silver has been found to be antiparasitic, antiviral, antibacterial and a powerful antioxidant. This combination has been reported to prevent candida overgrowth and give support to the immune and digestive systems. Colloidal Essence was formulated to provide maximum benefit by duplicating a high ppm rating frequency of colloidal silver and gold and the safety of a very low ppm rating of metallic silver and gold. This process ensures maximum strength and safety

ComforTone

This may aid in relieving complaints from constipation, bloating, gas and indigestion, as well as helping to remove toxic by-products from the body. It has also been reported to help the body dispel parasites and enhance colon function.

Femalin

This is an herbal and oil tincture formulated to help protect the female reproductive system from candida and degeneration. It has been reported to be very beneficial in getting rid of uterine and ovarian cysts.

FemiGen

This is an herbal formula, with nonanimal glandular substances and amino acids, which helps build and balance the reproductive system and maintain better hormonal balance for developmental years all the way through menopause. When one has experienced mood swings, P.M.S., and symptoms related to menopause, it is an indication that the body is nutritionally out of balance.

Gojo Berry Tea

This is a delicious-tasting antioxidant tea that may help support the immune system. The wolfberry is traditionally used in China to protect the body from cancer, liver and kidney problems, and as an antioxidant, it promotes longer life. It has been reported from various universities in China, Hong Kong, and Peru, that the plant Uncaria Tomentosa has been used to fight and prevent cancer and arthritis. Nopal, used in Mexico, has been tested and found to reduce cholesterol, burn fat, and prevent diabetes. Purple Lapacho has been reported to help support the body by cleansing the lymphatics, building blood cells and preventing disease. Ginseng, for thousands of years, has been used in the Orient to extend life and balance hormones. The oils of lemon, peppermint and spearmint help promote circulation and leukocyte formation.

HRT

This is a formula that was created out of specially selected herbs and oils to give nutritional support to help overcome deficiencies and irregularities of the heart.

I.C.P. Fiber Beverage

This is a unique source of fiber and bulk for the diet, which helps speed the transit time of waste matter through the intestinal tract. The psyllium, oat bran, flax and rice bran are balanced to eliminate allergy symptoms that may be experienced when taking psyllium alone. Essential oils enhance the flavor and may help dispel gas and discomfort.

ImmuGel

This is a unique blend of liquid amino acids, ionic charged trace minerals and herbal extracts with essential oils, creating one of nature's most powerful antioxidants and antimicrobial formulas. Amino acids have a unique ability to neutralize and help eliminate free radicals in the system.

ImmuneTune

This was created as a super antioxidant to support the body's immune defense system and fight against free radicals that are the primary cause of disease. The curcuminoid blend in this product has been found to be 60 percent stronger in antioxidant activity than pine bark or grape pit extract.. However, synergism is the key to obtaining maximum effect. Through the combining of 250 mg. per capsule of curcuminoids and 92 percent grape pit extract, we can increase the antioxidant frequency from 28 to 46 Hz. Pure DHEA is added as a very essential element in supporting the immune system and promoting longevity and strength. The minerals are added, which play an important part in maintaining cell electrolyte and PH balance. With chromium to support the metabolism and selenium to support the nervous system, its antioxidant ability adds to the synergism of the formula. With yucca and echineaca lending their support to the immune system, the antioxidant and anti-infectious attributes increase the nutrient support. The essential oil of orange increases the flavinoid activity; pine, fir, and thyme oils increase the anti-inflammatory action; and cistus adds its autoimmune support.

Immune Wolfberry Bar -
Nut 'N Berry Cinnamon - Nut 'N Berry Citrus.

The Wolfberry is a unique Chinese food that the Chinese have traditionally used as a liver and kidney tonic, and for building the immune system. It is believed that it extends life and promotes better health. At the universities in China, where much research has been conducted, the Wolfberry tests higher in Vitamin C than ascorbic acid, higher in beta carotene than carrots, and higher in amino acids than bee pollen. It has strong sweetening properties and when combined with stevia creates a most delicious and unique flavor in our Wolfberry Bar. Although there is a type of Wolfberry grown in America, the species that we are using, Lycium Chinese berry, is found only in China.

JuvaTone

This is a formula that plays a major role in helping the body to detoxify. The final products of digestion are transported through the portal vein from the colon to the liver to be cleansed. Another benefit that has been reported is that while taking JuvaTone, addictions to coffee, tea, tobacco, sugar, and alcohol are diminished. Many people have also found JuvaTone beneficial for reducing skin problems.

K & B

These herbs, combined with oils, have been used traditionally to help the kidneys and bladder in cases of irregularity, infection and bed-wetting.

Master Formula His - Hers - Children

This is a high-quality multivitamin, mineral, and amino acid supplement, which is formulated using a special sixteen-stage Synergistic Suspension Isolation. This process separates the antagonistic vitamins and herbs from the synergistic ones so they do not become abrasive and destroy each other. The Master Formula tablet has a special Zein coating derived from corn and the amino acid L-Phenylalaine enabling the body to recognize this supplement as a food, allowing for a faster conversion and assimilation.

HIS is formulated with more zinc and arginine, especially for men.

HERS is formulated with more magnesium, calcium and B vitamins to specifically help the special nutritional needs of women.

CHILDREN is a special **chewable** multivitamin formulated for children in the early growth years and for maintenance for adults in their later years. It is made with Chinese Wolfberry and grain proteins for added immune support, with beta carotene, vitamin C, amino acids and stevia.

Megazyme

This is a formula supplies enzymes to individuals who have difficulty digesting or assimilating food. Enzymes help digest toxic waste and gases from everyday metabolism, and retard the aging process.

Mineral Essence

This contains 80 plus ionic trace minerals. These minerals have the smallest molecular form, which facilitates their transmission across a lipid barrier (as in a cell membrane). Trace minerals are very vital elements of the human body. Without them, we would lose the electrolyte balance in our cells, which would contribute to premature aging and disease. Heart disease, which is the number one killer in America, may

160

start from a trace mineral deficiency in the smooth muscle of the heart. **Trace minerals play an important part in immune and metabolism functions.** For example, zinc carries out 200 enzyme functions and protects the prostate, skin, hair and nails. Magnesium has the responsibility of 300 enzyme functions, with many that are heart related. Trace minerals are as vital as oxygen. When combined with honey and royal jelly, they support blood sugar and help with energy and hormonal balance.

The fluids of the body are largely ionic. Ions regulate acid-base balance and water balance and serve essential roles in nerve condition, muscle contraction, heart action, blood clotting, protein metabolism, bone and tooth formation, and enzyme activation. In fact, every body process is dependent on ions. This action then becomes the energy source that initiates body functions ranging from muscle contraction to creative thought. The essential oil of cinnamon is antiviral, antibacterial and is a very powerful antioxidant containing high levels of phenols, which are the oxygenating molecules that work as a catalyst. Lemon promotes leukocyte production, which is an important function of the immune system. Peppermint is antibacterial and is a great support to the nervous system. These oils improve nutritional delivery and greatly enhance the taste of Mineral Essence.

Mint Condition

This is a combination of herbs and oils that may help to soothe an irritated digestive system, reduce inflammation and **improve digestive function.** It has been reported to help reduce ulcers, colitis, irritable bowel syndrome, bloating, gas and acid indigestion. It works harmoniously with Megazyme and Di-Tone. A good combination is to use Megazyme before meals and Mint Condition after meals.

ProGen

This is a new all-vegetable and herbal support for the male glandular system. The Pygeum Africanum has been used for years to prevent prostate atrophy and malfunction. With support from the total formula, we hope to see protection from prostate cancer and better glandular function. The oils used to flavor enhance this formula have been reported in Europe to also help support and prevent degeneration.

Progessence

This is a topical cream containing natural progesterone derived from soy added to flax seed, lecithin and vitamin E. This is combined with Siberian ginseng, black and blue cohosh and the essential oils of clary sage, sage, fennel, bergamot, ylang ylang and yarrow, which have traditionally been used to help the body produce the natural hormones of estrogen, testosterone and progesterone. It also contains wild Mexican yam, which has been widely recognized to produce natural estrogen and DHEA. Based on the research of John Lee, M.D., natural progesterone may help normalize thyroid function and blood sugar levels, improve bone density, increase metabolism, normalize cell oxygenation, enhance libido and diminish wrinkles. Dr. Lee also indicates that progesterone may be converted to estrogen if there is an estrogen deficiency. Progesterone supports hormonal balance, thus helping with PMS, hot flashes, headaches, asthma, backaches, infertility, inflammation, exhaustion, insomnia, arthritis, prostate problems and many others. It is best absorbed through the soft areas of the skin, such as inside the arms and thighs or as desired. Some may want to apply it once or twice daily while others may want to apply it only once or twice weekly.

Radex

Radex, as an antioxidant, was formulated with essential oils to help support the body in the prevention of free radical buildup from air pollution, chemicals and radiation and to increase oxygen in the system. The super oxide dismutase has been found to be a free radical scavenger.

Rehemogen

This contains herbs that were used by Chief Sundance and the native American Indians as a blood cleanser and builder, especially for blood-related and other degenerative diseases.

Royaldophilus

It is extremely important for acidophilus to implant on the intestinal wall for the culturing of intestinal flora. The problem with lactose intolerance is that the pasteurization of the milk before being cultured kills the enzymes. Our whole-milk acidophilus provides greater culture and inhibits allergy reactions. In our research, we found that plantain increases the culturing and bioavailability of the intestinal flora, helps to reduce digestive problems, and is very soothing to irritable bowel problem, where intestinal flora is absent. Although this product contains no essential oils, it is very beneficial to our digestive system and in preventing candida overgrowth.

Royal Essence

This tincture is a combination of herbs, minerals, amino acids, royal jelly and essential oils that help support the body and increase energy, endurance, and mental capacity. This product contains no caffeine or any other addicting properties. It has been found to help balance electrolytes and hormones, improve digestion, and is an excellent product for someone who is always on the go.

Stevia *(Stevia Rebaudiana Bertoni)*

Stevia has been used as a sweetener in South America for over 1500 years. It is 30 times sweeter than sugar and contains no calories. However, stevia has only been approved in the U.S. as a dietary supplement by the FDA since September 18, 1995. Scientific research has shown that stevia helps regulate both high and low blood sugar, increases energy and mental awareness, lowers elevated blood pressure and inhibits the growth of some bacteria and infections, including those that cause tooth decay and gum disease. Many people also taut the wonderful attributes of stevia for smoothing wrinkles and softening and beautifying the skin.

Super B

It is a powerful natural antioxidant. It is important to have a B-complex formula that can deliver all of the essential nutrients needed to support the body's cells, particularly in times of stress when assimilation is most difficult. Although this formula contains no essential oils, it is important for our bodies, as most diets are deficient in this vitamin, to have the B vitamins necessary for normal functions of immune response.

Super C

Super C is properly balanced with rutin, biotin, bioflavonoids and trace minerals to work synergistically, balancing the electrolytes, which increase the absorption rate of vitamin C. The essential oils may increase the oxygen and the bioflavonoid activity. This is a wonderful antioxidant.

Super Cal

This is a specially designed calcium, potassium and magnesium mineral supplement, which is important for proper hormonal balance and muscle and bone development. It has been found to help the nerves with stress and may help with and prevent hives.

Thyromin

This is a special blend of glandular nutrients, herbs, amino acids, minerals, herbs and essential oils perfectly balanced to bring about the most biological and nutritional support to the thyroid. This gland regulates body metabolism and temperature, and prevents fatigue, etc. It is therefore extremely important that it be healthy to function properly.

VitaGreen

This high-protein chlorophyll formula helps the body maintain a high energy level. It is made with a base of alfalfa sprouts that are 100% organic and are grown indoors. It may aid in cleansing the blood and supporting the immune system. Alfalfa sprouts, barley grass and spirulina have been reported to help balance blood sugar levels, alleviating a tired, run-down feeling. The essential oils in this formula may enhance immune function. VitaGreen is also beneficial for O blood-type vegetarians who need more protein.

Young Living Skin and Hair Care Products

Many of the skin and hair care products today contain harmful petrochemicals that cause allergic reactions and skin and scalp irritations. They use mineral oils that dehydrate the skin and sodium lauryl sulfate that causes allergies, dandruff and scalp rashes. Chemical molecules plug the pores of the skin, causing loss of oxygen and irritation.

The ancient Egyptians used fine vegetable oil as a carrier for the essential oils. Their small molecules are absorbed into the derma and subderma skin cells to kill bacteria, oxygenate, regenerate and rehydrate the cells. Skin care products, which are free of petrochemicals and animal products and are formulated with all-natural ingredients and essential oils, are the perfect products for maintaining beautiful, healthy skin.

Massage Oils

Massage or therapeutic touch has always been part of the healing for both physical and emotional needs. When essential oils are combined with massage, the benefits are numerous. It improves circulation and lymphatic drainage and aids in the elimination of tissue wastes. The oils create peace and tranquility while bringing about keen mental awareness. Massage opens and increases the flow of energy, balancing the entire nervous system and helping to release physical and emotional disharmony. The unrefined carrier vegetable oils are rich in fat-soluble nutrients and essential fatty acids, which are easily absorbed through the skin and utilized in the body.

Cel-Lite Magic

Cel-Lite Magic combines sesame seed oil, grape seed oil, sunflower seed oil, wheat germ oil and vitamin E with the essential oils of cedarwood, juniper, clary sage and pepper, which are reported to tone the skin. The oil of cypress enhances circulation, strengthens vascular walls, and decongests the lymphatic system. Orange and grapefruit oils are beneficial in dissolving cellulite.

Dragon Time

Improper diet and lifestyle changes are two of the things that can create severe hormone imbalances, resulting in PMS and premenopausal symptoms. European research has shown that the essential oils of clary sage, fennel, sage, jasmine and lavender, have each had beneficial results in helping to reduce some of these symptoms and correct imbalances. In addition to massage, it is soothing to put one-half ounce in the bathtub for a refreshing bath.

Ortho Ease

This massage oil has been used in European hospitals to help relieve muscle cramps and arthritic pain, and to give relief to sports injuries. The essential oils of birch, juniper, marjoram, red thyme, vetiver, peppermint, eucalyptus and lemongrass all assist with aches and pains.

Relaxation

This blends the essential oils of tangerine, rosewood, spearmint, peppermint, ylang ylang and lavender, which help us to relax and unwind, and has been reported to be beneficial for stress, muscle cramps and tension.

Sensation

This combines the exotic oils of ylang ylang, rosewood and jasmine. Sexual problems are an ever-increasing challenge today. The increased chemicals in our environment, air, food, water and stressful lifestyles all contribute to glandular and hormonal imbalance. Sensation leaves skin feeling silky and youthful, and its beautiful fragrance may stimulate feelings of romance and desire.

V-6 Mixing Oil

This combines food-grade vegetable oils for mixing with essential oils to create blends, formulas and massage oils. Grape seed oil, wheat germ oil and vitamin E are nurturing to the skin as natural antioxidants. V-6 is also excellent for cooking and making salad dressings.

Skin Cleansers

California Peach Facial Cleanser

This is a cleansing agent that contains the essential oils of rosewood, ylang ylang, rosemary and melaleuca that dispenses nutrients and oxygen to the skin. Peach and apricot oils cleanse pores and close them.

Mint Facial Scrub

This product eliminates layers of dead skin cells. Oatmeal and corn flour provide a mild abrasive texture that helps stimulate the pores, bringing oxygen to the surface to prevent premature aging of the skin cells. It is excellent for teenage skin, providing soothing relief to those with acne. This scrub can be used as a drying face mask to draw impurities from the skin. If the texture is too abrasive, it can be mixed with the California Peach Cleanser. The essential oils of lavender, melaleuca, palmarosa, peppermint, rosemary, rosewood and spearmint are a wonderful combination for cleaning and disinfecting the skin.

Moisturizers

Honeysuckle Rose Moisture Cream

This cream has the luxurious, refreshing fragrance of spring flowers, and is excellent for dry or prematurely aging skin. The essential oils of lavender, rose and rosewood are very beautifying to the skin and when combined with the fragrance of honeysuckle, gardenia and lilac create a wonderful scent.

Sensation Moisture Cream

This cream contains the exotic oils of jasmine, ylang ylang, rose and rosewood, which help maintain a youthful luster and exude a delicious, tantalizing fragrance.

Lotions and Creams

Genesis Hand and Body Lotion

This is a beautiful blend of coconut oil, lecithin and essential oils. It moisturizes, softens and protects your skin from harsh weather, work, chemicals, household cleaners, etc. The essential oils of rosewood, geranium, chamomile, patchouly, jasmine and rose penetrate and increase absorption, leaving the skin feeling smooth and when combined with honeysuckle and gardenia provide a beautiful fragrance.

Gentle Care Rose Ointment

This is a skin ointment containing sesame oil, lanolin, lecithin, vitamin E, beeswax, avocado, sweet almond, apricot, and grapeseed oils that feed and nourish the skin. These ingredients combined with the essential oils of rose seed, carrot seed, myrrh, rosemary, patchouly, rosewood and melaleuca supply nutrients that help slow down the aging process. It also assists in the healing of skin conditions; such as, psoriasis, diaper rash, chapped skin and poison oak or ivy.

Sensation Hand and Body Lotion

This soothing lotion is delightful to wear with its intoxicating combination of rosewood, ylang ylang, jasmine and rose. It leaves the skin soft and moist as it protects the skin from harsh weather, chemicals and dry air.

Sunsation Suntan Oil

This product contains coconut oil, cocoa butter, aloe vera, mink oil, wheat germ oil, and vitamin E that help filter out the ultraviolet rays without blocking the absorption of vitamin D. This is important in skin and bone development. The essential oils of lavender, melaleuca, lemongrass and citronella accelerate tanning and act as a natural insect repellent. There are no chemicals or additives in Sunsation. It has a 6 SPF rating.

Shampoos and Conditioners

Our shampoos are made from the most natural products possible: vegetable oil and lecithin for lather, panthenol and panthetine to strengthen and feed the hair shaft, and herbal extracts to clean the hair and scalp. Selected essential oils carry the nutrients to the hair follicles and subdermal cells to improve hair texture as well as to protect the hair and scalp from exposure to chemicals, hair spray, permanents and coloring. They are formulated in a base of water, castile, cocodiethanolamine, algenic acid, panethol, vegetable glycerine, aloe vera, nettle extract, birch bark extract, biotin, floral water, jojoba, safflower, avocado and wheat germ.

Apple Blossom Shampoo

This is a multipurpose shampoo. The essential oils of rosemary, lavender, rosewood and juniper create a springtime scent. It is perfect for every member of the family, including babies.

Lavender Shampoo

This may help prevent hair loss, promote hair growth and reduce dandruff and scalp rashes. The essential oils of lavender, rosemary, juniper, cedarwood, clary sage, and ylang ylang make this a favorite shampoo for everyone.

Rosewood Mist Shampoo and Conditioner

This contains the essential oils of rosewood, palmarosa, sage, lavendin, clary sage, rose, patchouly and ylang ylang, making it a great combination for hard-to-manage dry hair, split ends and damaged hair from perms, hair coloring and bleaches.

Silken Essence Conditioner

This conditioner leaves your hair silky and smooth. It contains egg biotin, olive and avocado oils, nettle extract, henna and the essential oils of sage, rosemary, ylang ylang, yarrow, patchouly, clary sage, rosewood, cedarwood and lavender, that act as a moisturizer that not only protects the hair but leaves it shiny and manageable. The ingredients have been used in Egypt for hair care for thousands of years.

Bath and Shower Gels

Algin, olive oil, vegetable glycerine, floral water, vitamin E, lecithin, wheat germ and essential oils create a synergistic action for cleansing and stimulating subdermal and dermal cells. They nourish and replenish the nutrients necessary for skin and cell regeneration. The essential oils in these formulas allow our skin to breathe and assimilate more oxygen, which is the key to maintaining youthful cells.

Dragon Time Bath & Shower Gel

This was blended for that time of the month that leaves women with lower back pain, stress and sleeping difficulties. The essential oils of clary sage, fennel, lavender and jasmine work well together and are soothing and uplifting both physically and emotionally.

Evening Peace Bath and Shower Gel

This blends the essential oils of blue chamomile, clary sage, lavender, rosewood, rose and ylang ylang, which relax tired, fatigued muscles, and help alleviate stress and tension.

Morning Start Bath & Shower Gel

This is an invigorating gel that combines the essential oils of lemongrass, cypress, rosemary, juniper and peppermint, giving you a fresh start to your day with the surge of energy needed in today's fast-paced world.

Sensation Bath & Shower Gel

This contains the oils used by Cleopatra to enhance love and increase desire to be close to that someone special. The essential oils of rosewood, ylang ylang, jasmine and rose create an enchanting fragrance.

Bath Gel Base

This contains the natural ingredients of olive oil, vegetable glycerine, floral water, algine vitamin E, lecithin and wheat germ for cleansing the pores of the skin. You can add Singles and Blends to create the fragrance or therapeutic action desired. It is fun to be able to create your own fragrance for gifts for family and friends.

Cologne and Aftershave

Pharaoh and Rawhide Aftershave

This contains no alcohol or petrochemicals that contribute to allergies and that dry, burning feeling. Shaving opens the pores and dehydrates the skin. Pharaoh and Rawhide both moisturize, rehydrate and replenish oxygen to the skin to help retard the aging process. These lotions are soothing, cooling and refreshing.

Pharaoh

Pharaoh is rich and exotic with the essential oil of cedarwood and the fragrances of orange blossom and musk, creating a very unique and regal aroma.

Rawhide

This lotion combines the essential oil of ylang ylang with the fragrances of lilac and honeysuckle, emanating the scent of the mountains and the desert.

Bibliography

Becker, M.D., Robert O. *The Body Electric.* New York: Wm. Morrow, 1985.

Belaiche, M.D., Paul. *Traité de Phytothérapie Et D'Aromathérapie.* Paris: Maloine, 1979.

Belvi, Viktor. *Aromatherapy.* New York: Avon Books, 1993.

The *Bible.* King James Version. Books from Old and New Testament.

Burrows, Stanley. *Healing for the Age of Enlightenment.* Kailoua, Hawaii, 1976.

Chopra, M.D., Deepak. *Quantum Healing.* New York: Bantam Books, 1989.

Darom, David. *Beautiful Plants of the Bible.* Israel: Palphot, Ltd.

Doss, Besada. *The Story of Abu Simbel.* Essex, England: Longman Group UK Limited, 1973.

Farag, Ph.D., Radwan S. "Safety Evaluation of Thyme and Clove Essential Oils as Natural Antioxidants." *African Journal of Agricultural Sciences, Vol. 18, No. 1.* Gisa, Egypt: Cairo University, 1991.

Gattefossé, Ph.D., René-Maurice. *Aromatherapy.* Paris: Girardot, 1937.

Garrison, Omar. *Tantra: The Yoga of Sex.* New York: Harmony Books, 1964.

Guenther, Ernest. *The Essential Oils.* Malabar, Florida, 1950.

LaDoux, M.D., Joseph. *Rationalizing Thoughtless Emotions.* Insight, Sept. 1989.

Mailhebiau, Philippe. *La Nouvelle Aromathérapie.* Editions. France: Jakin, 1994.

Masquelier, J. *Radical Scavenging Effect of Proanthocyanidins.* Paris, 1986.

Maury, Marguerite. *The Secret of Life and Youth* (Guide to Aromatherapy). Great Britain: McDonald & Co., 1964.

Meunier, Christiane. *Lavandes & Lavandins.* Aix-en-Provence, France: Chaudoreille, 1985.

Momchilova, A. M. *330 Years of Bulgarian Rose Oil.* Sofia, Bulgaria, 1994.

Niazi, H. *The Egyptian Prescription.* Cairo, Egypt: Elias Modern Press, 1988.

Nordenstrom, Bjorn. *Biologically Closed Circuits.* Sweden.

Pénoël, M.D., Daniel and Pierre Franchomme. *L'aromathérapie exactement.* Limoges, France: Jollois, 1990.

Plato. *Chronicles 156 e.*

Restick, M.D., Richard. *The Brain.* New York: Random House, 1991.

Ryman, Daniele. *Aromatherapy, The Complete Guide to Plant and Flower Essences for Health and Beauty.* New York: Bantam Books, 1993.

Valnet, M.D., Jean. *Aromathérapie.* Rochester, Vermont: Healing Arts Press, 1982.

Williams, David. *Lecture Notes.* London, England, 1988.